5-MINUTE
CALM

5-MINUTE
CALM

A More Peaceful, Rested, and Relaxed You in Just 5 MINUTES A DAY

Adams Media

New York   London   Toronto   Sydney   New Delhi

Adams Media
An Imprint of Simon & Schuster, Inc.
57 Littlefield Street
Avon, Massachusetts 02322

First Adams Media trade paperback edition JANUARY 2018

ADAMS MEDIA and colophon are trademarks of Simon and Schuster.

For information about special discounts for bulk purchases, please contact Simon & Schuster Special Sales at 1-866-506-1949 or business@simonandschuster.com.

The Simon & Schuster Speakers Bureau can bring authors to your live event. For more information or to book an event contact the Simon & Schuster Speakers Bureau at 1-866-248-3049 or visit our website at www.simonspeakers.com.

Interior design by Michelle Kelly

Manufactured in the United States of America

10 9 8 7 6 5 4 3 2 1

Library of Congress Cataloging-in-Publication Data has been applied for.

ISBN 978-1-5072-0630-0
ISBN 978-1-5072-0631-7 (ebook)

Many of the designations used by manufacturers and sellers to distinguish their products are claimed as trademarks. Where those designations appear in this book and Simon & Schuster, Inc., was aware of a trademark claim, the designations have been printed with initial capital letters.

This book is intended as general information only and should not be used to diagnose or treat any health condition. In light of the complex, individual, and specific nature of health problems, this book is not intended to replace professional medical advice. The ideas, procedures, and suggestions in this book are intended to supplement, not replace, the advice of a trained medical professional. Consult your physician before adopting any of the suggestions in this book, as well as about any condition that may require diagnosis or medical attention. The author and publisher disclaim any liability arising directly or indirectly from the use of this book.

Contains material adapted from the following titles published by Adams Media, an Imprint of Simon & Schuster, Inc.: *Meditation for Moms* by Kim Dwyer and Susan Reynolds, copyright © 2012, ISBN 978-1-4405-3027-2; *365 Ways to Reduce Stress* by Eve Adamson, copyright © 2009, ISBN 978-1-4405-0025-1; and *Meditation Made Easy* by Preston Bentley, copyright © 2015, ISBN 978-1-4405-8432-9.

CONTENTS

PART 3
Calm Your Life 195

INTRODUCTION

Calmness—it's such a simple concept, yet it is something many of us have a hard time achieving in this busy world. Calmness gives you a renewed sense of self, an improved outlook on life, and relief for tense and tight muscles. You deserve to take time for yourself each day to experience the healing properties of calmness.

5-Minute Calm will help you regain your sense of peace. In this book, you'll find over two hundred quick and simple ways to calm the tension and stress around you and feel the rejuvenating power of calmness. You may think you are too busy to take some time for yourself, but all you need is 5 minutes or less to release the pressures of life and find tranquility. From meditations that will clear your mind and yoga postures that will relax your muscles to enjoyable activities that will refresh your spirit, this book will be your guide to cutting out the noise and stress of life and reminding you just how perfect calmness can feel.

When the worries of the day begin to wear on you, open this book to any page and find a sense of calm.

PART 1
CALM YOUR MIND

BREATH CONTROL, STEP BY STEP

Deep, slow breathing begins to work almost immediately, but still, it is something you'll get better at the more you practice. Try this:

1. In the beginning, try inhaling for 8 seconds, holding for 4 seconds, exhaling for 8 seconds, and holding for 4 seconds.
2. For deliberate practice, start with 5 minutes of breath work each morning and evening and gradually increase from there. In addition, anytime you feel anxious, do a few repetitions to calm yourself.
3. Build to inhaling for 12 seconds, holding for 6 seconds, exhaling for 12 seconds, and holding for 6 seconds. This will become the foundation of your relaxation practice.

See how manageable breath control can be? You can do it in line at the supermarket, while driving, or while sitting at your desk. To get the full effect, though, you will want to devote a few minutes each day to exclusively focusing on breathing. Feel your lungs expand and contract. Watch your breath flow in and out. Count mentally as you go. Once you have the rhythm down, you can stop counting and just concentrate on the breath.

CLEAR YOUR MIND THROUGH DEEP BREATHING

One of the best and most often used ways to calm your mind is through deep breathing. Deep breathing is different from your usual automatic breathing—deep breaths allow you to clear your mind and give yourself an opportunity to see your thoughts. Here's how to do it:

1. Count from one to five as you breathe in. Don't worry about breath control for now; just breathe normally. Concentrate on just the numbers one through five.
2. As soon as your mind begins to wander, start over again at one. If you think about what you might have for lunch or the next item on your agenda, start over at one. You may find yourself rarely—if ever—making it to five.
3. If you do make it to five, start over again at one. Avoid the temptation to count while simultaneously thinking of other things, as this defeats the purpose of the exercise.

Notice how, at first, your mind flits from topic to topic in perpetual activity? With practice, you'll be able to stop that cycle. You'll instead be able to "watch" your thoughts as they arise. You will feel a sensation of opening, as if you're creating mental space. Indeed, the reason we don't have more peace in our lives is because we don't create space for peace—we crowd it out, externally and internally.

CLEAR YOUR MIND THROUGH OBSERVATION

When you find yourself able to calm your mind, you can start consciously observing your thoughts and emotions. If you feel angry or sad about something, think objectively about that emotion...and its associated words, images, and feelings. This kind of introspection should be kept free and light. You're not psychoanalyzing yourself. You need not form any opinions about the images, thoughts, memories, and plans that arise in your mind—just accept that they're there. If you find yourself spinning downward in a negative chain of thought, gently bring yourself back to your calm center.

One way to clear your mind is to become aware of your surroundings: for 5 minutes, listen to the subtle sounds around you. All silence is really composed of minute amounts of noise. If you are in an office, listen to the ventilation system or the hum of electric lights. It may sound silly, but these can become sacred sounds if you associate them with a calm mind. If you are outside, listen to the sounds of birds and feel the sensation of the breeze on your skin.

Breathe deeply with your eyes open so that you can take in your surroundings. Again, don't judge or analyze your surroundings—just notice and accept them. Encouraging yourself to notice details around you is an effective way to quiet your own mind.

IMAGINE POSITIVE CHANGES

Imagery meditation uses your imagination to make positive changes in your thinking. The purpose of imagery meditation is to imagine yourself in a different place (the beach, Paris, etc.) or different circumstances to effect instant relaxation. Imagining gives you instant stress relief because of the positive feelings you associate with what you are visualizing.

Even if your imagination is a little rusty, you can practice imagery meditation. It's fun! No matter what is causing you stress, this imagination-generating exercise is a powerful stress management technique, both in the short and long term. Here is how to practice imagery meditation:

1. Get comfortable, either sitting or lying down.
2. Close your eyes. Take a few deep, relaxed breaths, then form a picture in your mind. Maybe it is a place you wish you could be right now, a place you visited in the past and loved, or a place you invent.
3. What does the place look like? What do you see around you? What colors, what textures? Notice everything about the place you are visualizing.
4. Then, imagine touching things around you: sand, water, grass, trees, great art or architecture, your favorite person.

5. Listen. What do you hear in this place?
6. Next, think about what you smell.
7. Focus on each of your senses and explore the place you've created or remembered in your mind.
8. Stay here as long as you like, but for at least 5 minutes. Then, slowly, let the images fade away and open your eyes.

VISUALIZE THE CHANGES YOU WANT

Another way to use your imagination to improve your life is to visualize the changes you want to make in your life. You'll find that the more you practice this exercise, the more the things in your life will change for the better. Why? Because continually visualizing something can help bring about those changes. Here's how to do it:

1. Get comfortable, either sitting or lying down.
2. Close your eyes. Take a few deep, relaxed breaths, then form a picture in your mind of some kind of positive life change. Maybe it's a career goal or a change in your health or appearance, situation, confidence, or anything else. Keep it simple and stick to one thing. You can always tackle other areas in separate sessions.
3. Imagine yourself in your new situation. How do you look, act, feel? How do you like being this way, looking like this, having this job?
4. If you like it and it feels right, then continue this visualization for at least 5 minutes every day. Imagine it with fervent and confident intention.

Be Flexible with Visualization

As your life changes, your visualizations may change and grow. You may realize, for example, that as your life becomes less stressful and more rewarding, you don't really need to be financially wealthy, because you have gained emotional and spiritual wealth instead. The trick is to continue visualizing. The more you use your imagination, the stronger it becomes, just like a muscle.

To add power to your visualization, use an affirmation as a mantra for your meditation, worded positively, as if the change has already taken place (rather than saying "I won't be sick," say "I will be well"). Use the affirmation as a mantra while you visualize your goal.

LEARN ABOUT MINDFULNESS MEDITATION

Mindfulness meditation can be practiced anywhere, anytime, no matter what you are doing. It is simply focusing on total awareness of the present moment. Anything you are doing, you can do with mindfulness.

Mindfulness meditation is easy to do for short periods, like 5 minutes. It is tough to do for an extended time because our minds resist staying in the present moment, but it is a rewarding mental discipline that teaches us to cherish and relish the miracle of the present moment no matter how ordinary the moment is. Mindfulness meditation is also supremely relaxing and satisfying. Here is how to practice mindfulness meditation:

- Wherever you are, you can practice mindfulness meditation by consciously making the decision to be fully aware of everything around you.
- Notice the impressions from all your senses: see, hear, feel, smell, taste.
- When your mind begins to think about something else, gently bring it back to the present moment. You may be amazed at what you notice about yourself and the world around you.

If practicing mindfulness anywhere sounds overwhelming, you can start practicing it while doing something very specific, like eating. Pick a single thing to eat—a vegetable, a piece of fruit, or a piece of bread. Eat it slowly, and notice everything about the process. How do you bring the food to your mouth? How does it feel? How does it taste and smell? Practicing mindfulness meditation while eating is a good way to hone your mindfulness skills. It is also a way to help overcome mindless eating.

OBJECT MEDITATION

This meditation can help quiet your mind and bring your focus back to you. Find an object that is beautiful or interesting to you. It can be a shell or a religious icon or a piece of your mother's jewelry or a perfume bottle she gave you that you always loved. Choose anything that is meaningful to you.

1. Place the object in front of you, positioned so that you are able to be seated with your eyes gazing forward at the object.
2. Keep your eyes focused on the object without looking away.
3. Begin to breathe deeply, transitioning into long, slow breaths that you draw deeply into your belly, slowly and fully.
4. Keep your every thought on the physical aspects of the object—its texture, size, color... All your awareness rests on the physical aspects of the object. When your mind wanders, notice what it wanders to, then bring it back to the object.
5. Once you feel calm and focused, close your eyes and try to "see" the object in your mind's eye. If you lose your concentration, open your eyes, study the object, and then try again.

Stay with this meditation for 5 minutes or for as long as you'd like.

SAY RELAX

Try this simple meditation to calm your mind: simply follow your breath and anchor it to a word or phrase.

- Inhale and say "Peace."
- Exhale and say "Relax."
- Inhale... "Peace."
- Exhale... "Relax."

Have no agenda—just the breath.

This quick meditation may seem almost too simple, but the results can be significant in terms of releasing stress, slowing down, and centering yourself.

OPEN YOUR MIND TO PRAYER

Prayer is a focused, concentrated communication, statement of intention, or opening of the channel between you and divinity, whatever divinity is for you. A prayer can be a request, thanks, worship, or praise to God. It can be an intention of being thankful directed to the universe. It can be used to invoke divine power or as an attempt to experience divine or universal energy directly. There are many different traditions and each has its own modes and types of prayer. Prayer can mean whatever you want it to mean. Here is a practice prayer to try:

1. First decide to whom, to what, or toward whom or what your prayer is addressed.
2. Next, think about the substance of your prayer. Are you praying for healing for yourself or someone else? Are you praying for something you want or need? Are you praying to say thank you for everything you already have?
3. Once you have a specific intention in mind, sit or lie quietly in a place where you are unlikely to be disturbed.
4. Focus your thought on your prayer and say it, either out loud or in your mind.
5. Stay focused on your prayer and the energy of your prayer. Imagine where it is going. Let your prayer continue to radiate from your heart toward its intended source.

TAP INTO A LITTLE MANTRA MOJO

A science called Naad holds that the roof of your mouth has eighty-four meridian points (located along energy channels) that can be stimulated when your tongue strikes them, such as when you're speaking. According to Naad, the meridian points stimulate the hypothalamus gland, which stimulates the pineal gland, which stimulates the pituitary gland. The pituitary gland and the entire glandular system play a role in experiencing emotions and achieving bliss, which means that the sound of a word (and the meridian the tongue strikes while saying the word) is just as important as what the word means. Over thousands of years, yogis have created mantras designed to strike meridians that will facilitate a meditative state.

Pronounced as it is spelled, *Om Mani Padme Hum*, one of the most popular mantras in the world, is intended to create compassion. Many people will begin saying it and transition into singing it, formulating their own tune. Roughly translated, it means "When the heart and the mind get together and combine efforts, then anything is possible." So whenever you need some mantra mojo, try saying and then chanting (or singing) "Om Mani Padme Hum...Om Mani Padme Hum" for 5 minutes and see how you feel.

PRACTICE MANTRA MEDITATION

Mantra meditation disciplines the mind, sharpens the focus, and even improves the depth of the breath and the capacity of the lungs. It's also supremely relaxing. Any focused concentration done while repeating a sound can be called a mantra meditation, whether it's Sufi chanting or the recitation of the rosary prayer. If you choose a word or phrase that means something to you, you may feel your meditation has a more personalized feel to it. Your mantra can even be an affirmation like "I am happy." Any word or phrase will do, but here are a few you might try if you don't already have something in mind:

- "Om"
- "Sky"
- "Peace"
- "Love"
- "Joy"
- "Earth"

Practice Mantra Meditation
- To practice mantra meditation, find a quiet place to sit. Get situated, centered, and in a comfortable position.
- Take a few relaxed breaths, then slowly begin to repeat your mantra with every exhalation of your breath.
- Repeat for 2 minutes at first, then build up to 5 minutes once or (if possible) twice each day.

LIMIT THE NOISE

One of the issues with today's world is noise—we are constantly bombarded with news, politics, and social media on our countless technological devices. It can be difficult to find some quiet time to calm your mind.

Like anything else, technology and media are fine...in moderation. But as with anything else, too much of a good thing soon becomes a bad thing. If your media habit is taking up more than its fair share of your time and you are sacrificing other, equally important or more important parts of your life because of your media fixation, then it's a bad habit. Also, if engaging in your media habit tends to make you feel down, angry, or gives you anxiety about the state of the world, it is critical to make time each day to turn it off. Seek balance in your media habit.

The noise habit is related to the media habit: if you always have to have a TV or radio on, or if you always fall asleep to TV or music, then you probably have a noise habit.

Noise can temporarily mask loneliness or nervousness. It can calm an anxious mind or distract a troubled one. Constant noise can provide a welcome relief from oneself, but if noise is compromising your ability to think and perform as well as you could, if noise is keeping you from confronting your stress and yourself, then it's time to make some space for silence in your life. Too much noise is stressful for the body and mind.

The solution is simple: give yourself a break and let yourself experience silence at least once each day for at least 5 minutes. Turn off your electronics and devices and just enjoy the silence. It isn't hard to do, and you'll notice that you will feel calmer even after just 5 minutes.

MEDITATE ON AN INTENTION

Go to someplace that is soothing in your home. Sit cross-legged on a folded blanket. Make sure your spine is lengthened. Before you begin, set an intention. (An intention can be thought of as a prayer.)

1. Once you formulate your intention, close your eyes and relax your jaw by parting your teeth. Only your lips will be touching.
2. Bring your hands, palms facing upward, onto your knees. (This hand gesture is done with the intention of receiving wisdom from the universe—or from God, if you prefer.)
3. Anchor your breath to a phrase, such as something from your intention. As you breathe, keep repeating your intention.
4. Inhale... Say your intention.
5. Exhale... Say your intention.

Try this for 5 minutes, setting a timer or an alarm so you won't be distracted by watching a clock.

After the timer goes off, sit in stillness, recognizing that an intention is powerful and that you can have faith and trust in the process. Notice how calm you feel. Savor this moment.

DO A ONE-BREATH MEDITATION

Everyday life continually poses challenges to your inner peace. In the midst of a stressful episode, whether at home or at work, you may long for the peaceful moments that quiet meditation offers. But the real world doesn't offer such moments when they're most needed—instead, you have to create them. At these times, a conscious pause can refresh your body and mind just as well as an extended meditation session can. Here's how to do it:

1. If you find yourself particularly stressed and feeling that you've come to the end of your rope, stop. Remind yourself that this is an opportune time to do momentary meditation to refresh and relax your mind.
2. Pause all thoughts and remind yourself that your inner peace is prevailing at this moment. Think of that peace as a place within you. Straighten your spine as you do this and lift your chin upward. Focus your eyes above your head, either at the ceiling or wall.
3. Take a conscious breath, slowly and deliberately. Think of your place of peace opening its door as the air fills your lungs. Upon exhaling, appreciate the moment for allowing you to pause, then return to the work at hand.

KEEP A JOURNAL

Feeling stressed? Create a stress journal. Sit in a quiet place with just your journal and a pen and no other distractions for 5 minutes and write. List your habits, describe what you think triggers them, and write down how each habit causes you stress. For example, you might write "nail biting" in the habits column, "feeling nervous or bored" in the triggers column, and "social embarrassment, feeling unattractive, annoyance at myself" in the causes-of-stress column. You don't have to spend hours berating yourself for your bad habits—just take 5 minutes out of your day to write down something you feel is adding to your stress.

Even if you aren't quite ready to give up a habit (perhaps you know you are addicted to TV, for example, but you aren't ready to quit watching your favorite shows just yet), record your habit in the chart anyway. You can deal with it when you are ready, even if you won't be ready any time soon. At least you'll have all your bad habits officially identified in one place.

PRACTICE THE PAUSE

People form bad habits—that just happens. None of us is perfect. But how can you break out of the bad-habit rut? Practice the pause. Be aware of your habit, and when you are about to fall into your habitual behavior, learn to pause just for a moment and think. Ask yourself these questions:

- Will this nourish my body?
- Will this nourish my spirit?
- Is this good for me?
- Will I feel good about doing this later? Or will I feel guilty about it later?
- Is it really worth the momentary pleasure?

More often than not, you will find yourself moving away from your bad habit once you have paused to think about it.

STAND AND MEDITATE

You may find yourself in a time or place where traditional sitting meditation is not possible. If that is the case, standing meditation is quite effective, and although it may not be comfortable for extended periods, it is perfect for a 5-minute calm down.

Here's how to do it properly:

1. Stand with your spine upright and your shoulders straight. This isn't an extremely rigid military stance—that would be tiring. Instead, your shoulders should be evenly balanced on both sides, and your chin should be tilted slightly upward but not stretched.
2. Stand with your feet about 12 inches apart and balance your weight evenly over your feet.
3. Place your hands at your sides with your palms against your thighs. Alternatively, you may find it more comfortable to hold both hands close to the center of your body with your palms inward. Do not cross or fold your arms.

You are now ready to meditate.

SEND LOVE

You can increase your calm by spreading it to others, making a calming ripple effect. You can send a feeling of love to a loved one at any time and from any place (as long as it is quiet). You can either sit or stand, assuming that you're able to lengthen your spine.

- When you are ready, take a few deep breaths, close your eyes, and quiet your mind. Think about the other person. If it's a new date, think about the thrill of attraction and interest. If it's a friend, re-member times you've laughed together. If it's your partner, think about the day you moved in together or your wedding day.
- Breathe in as you open your heart center: raise your shoulders up by your ears, then lower them down and back, gently pressing your shoulder blades closer together.
- Exhale, holding an image of your companion in your heart as you say these words:

May my heart be open to receive you and to connect with your heart.

May my eyes see you with a childlike delight.

May we enjoy each other's company, tonight and every night.

- Hold thoughts of love and light as you take a few more deep breaths...and then go enjoy your night.

TRY BREATHING MEDITATION

Breathing meditation is part *zazen* and part *pranayama*, which are the breathing techniques associated with yoga. In *zazen*, you watch your breath without judging, following it in and out. In *pranayama*, you control the length and character of the inhalation and exhalation. Breathing constantly infuses our body with oxygen and, according to some traditions, life-force energy. Here is how to practice it:

1. First, practice breathing deeply. Then, when you feel you can breathe from the lower part of your body rather than from your upper chest, sit comfortably, either on the floor or in a chair. Sit up straight so that you aren't scrunching up your body's breathing space. Imagine you are being held up from above so that the effort of sitting up straight feels effortless.

2. Now, take a long, slow, deep breath through your nose. At the same time, in your mind, count slowly to five. When you've inhaled fully at five, hold the breath for five more counts, then slowly release the breath through your nose for a count of ten. As you breathe and count, your mind will need to concentrate on the counting. At this point, it's time to focus on the sound and feel of the breath. Focus completely on the breath.

3. Keep breathing in this way for 5 minutes. If you enjoy this practice, you can increase your breathing meditation time by 2 minutes per week until you've reached 15 to 30 minutes once or twice each day.

LEARN ABOUT MANDALA MEDITATION

In mandala meditation (which comes from Tibetan culture), the focus of the meditation is placed on a beautiful object: a mandala. Mandalas are circular pictures—sometimes very plain, sometimes highly ornate—used for meditation. The round outer form and often the inner lines of the picture draw the eye to the center of the mandala, helping the mind focus on that center point. Mandalas are thought to be a symbolic representation of the universe, making them the perfect point of focus.

First, you need a mandala. You can find mandalas in books, in stores that carry imported items from Tibet, or those that carry meditation supplies. Or you can make one yourself. Then follow these steps:

1. Hang or place the mandala just below eye level from a sitting position. Sit 4 to 8 feet away from it, depending on how comfortable you feel. Sit cross-legged, in a kneeling position, or on a small bench or chair. If sitting on the floor, use a cushion to make yourself more comfortable.
2. Take a few relaxed breaths, then look at the mandala. Instead of following your breath or a sound, use the mandala as your point of concentration. Examine it in detail.
3. Practice for just 5 minutes once or twice each day. If you like this practice, you can add 2 minutes every week until you are up to 15 to 30 minutes of mandala meditation.

GIVE A GIFT

Another way to share your gratitude is to pay it forward: to perform small acts of kindness toward other people. Gifts can be anything. For example, you could buy someone's coffee ahead of you in the coffee line. Just tell the cashier, "That woman's coffee is on me," and then smile at the person and wish her a great day. It feels really good to give gifts.

You could pick some flowers from your garden and take them to a neighbor. You could offer someone your seat on the bus. If you have children, encourage them to do the same. As children watch your gift-giving, they will want to "help" people to smile as well. This gift-giving practice may last their entire lives.

The gift-giving experience can be a way to find deeper meaning in life. Think of gifts that do not cost any money: a smile for a stranger, holding a door open for someone, or helping someone put groceries in her car. In just a few minutes, you could give a gift for no reason at all that could have a profound impact on someone else's life.

JOURNAL YOUR DREAMS

While "the stuff dreams are made of" is still a matter of some controversy, many people believe that dreams tap the subconscious mind's hopes, fears, goals, worries, and desires.

Dream journaling is a way to begin keeping track of the images, themes, motifs, and emotions in your dreams. Because it helps you to work on your own mind and train your mind to dream in a beneficial way, dream journaling is a good stress management tool. This kind of mental training helps the mind become more resilient to stress.

First, find a journal you like that is pleasing to write in. Also, find a pen you enjoy writing with. Keep these items in a place you can reach while lying in bed. When you are in bed and ready to go to sleep, close your eyes and tell yourself: "I will remember my dreams tonight." This sets your intention in your mind. It may not work the first night, the second night, or even for a few weeks. But eventually, it should work.

In the morning, the second you wake up, reach for your dream journal and immediately start writing. If you remember a dream, write about it in as much detail as you can. Even if you don't remember a dream, just start writing whatever impression is in your head. As you write, dream impressions—even full dreams with elaborate plots—may come into your head. If they don't, you'll still be writing from the subconscious, which is more accessible in the first few minutes after awakening.

Then, after a month has passed, go back and read your journal. Do you see themes, motifs, recurring images? These are probably signals from your subconscious. Reflect on what they might be telling you about the direction of your life, your health, your relationships, and your happiness.

SEE THE GLASS AS HALF FULL

Have you been feeling a bit pessimistic? It happens to all of us—we all have bad days. Can you change your pessimism? Yes. You just need to engage in a little optimism therapy. Studies show that smiling even when you aren't happy can make you feel happy. Pretending to be an optimist can actually make you feel like one, too, and can help your body learn to respond like an optimist.

If your pessimism is temporary or recent, you can probably help yourself through your own personal optimism therapy sessions. At the beginning of each day, before you get out of bed, say one of these affirmations out loud several times:

- "No matter what happens today, I won't judge myself."
- "Today I will enjoy myself in healthy ways."
- "No matter what happens around me, this will be a good day."

Then, choose one part of your day and vow to be an optimist for 5 minutes during that time. Maybe you'll choose lunchtime, or the staff meeting, or the time with your kids before dinner. During that period, every time you begin to think or say something pessimistic, immediately replace those words or thoughts with something optimistic.

GET OUT OF THAT NEGATIVE-THINKING RUT

Negativity is a huge drain on your energy and exacerbates any stress in your life, magnifying it until it seems huge and uncontrollable. Many people are in the negativity habit. It may be a habit brought on by lots of past suffering, which is perfectly understandable. Still, though, the negativity can stop right now—even when you're suffering, you don't have to be negative. After all, some people remain positive through tragedy, while others despair. What's the difference? Attitude.

Identify Negativity Triggers

Once you know what kinds of things trigger your negativity, you can begin to catch yourself in the act. When something unexpected happens, do the first words out of your mouth tend to be a frantic "Oh, no!"? If so, stop yourself after that first "Oh–". Notice what you are doing. Say to yourself, "I don't have to respond this way. I should wait and see if a full-blown, all-out 'Oh, no!' is really warranted." This stopping of your thought process and your negative reaction can help you be more objective and eventually more positive about any situation. Even if you've stopped yourself and then realize that an "Oh, no!" really *is* warranted, you won't be crying wolf at every little mishap.

Kick the Negativity Habit

Just like any habit, the more you get used to halting your negative reactions and replacing them with neutral or positive reactions, the less you'll find yourself reacting negatively to begin with. Instead of "Oh, no!" react with silence, taking a wait-and-see attitude. Or react with an affirmation: "Oh...I can learn something positive from this!"

You might encounter obstacles along the way; that's to be expected. But even if a negative attitude is comforting in some ways, is it worth the drain on your energy and happiness? Keep working through it—you'll get there.

TRY *SHAMATHA*

Shamatha means calm abiding, tranquility, or meditation. All you are doing in this exercise is watching breathing—no more, no less. This breath-watching will, even within just 5 minutes, calm the nervous system and bring a feeling of peace. Let's take a few minutes to pay attention to the breath.

1. Close your eyes. Close your mouth.
2. Notice the length of each in-breath. If your in-breaths are only 2 or 3 seconds long, they are shallow breaths, a surefire sign that you're stressed.
3. Notice the temperature of your breath. Is it cool when you inhale and warm when you exhale?
4. Notice the direction of your breath. When you inhale, can you feel your breath filling your lungs and causing your belly to expand? Can you feel your breath entering your nose and cooling the inside of your nose and then passing downward into your lungs?
5. After bringing all this awareness to your breath as it is, slowly begin to inhale longer and deeper. You want each in-breath to be about 5 or 6 seconds long and the exhale to be an equal length of time.

6. Bring your right hand to your belly. Breathe deeply (5 or 6 seconds), drawing in air until your belly presses into your hand. As you exhale, let your navel sink until it is pressing toward your spine.

7. Continue breathing in and out as you begin to count the breath: one, two, three, four, five for the in-breath and five, four, three, two, one for the exhale. If counting seems too boring, say a mantra, such as "May I have peace" as you inhale and "May all have peace" as you exhale.

MANAGE INTRUSIVE THOUGHTS

Instead of trying to push thoughts out of the way when they try to interrupt your calm, you can make a meditation out of viewing them in a detached, disengaged manner. You can do this by neutralizing them. Here's how it works:

- If a distracting thought comes forward, view it as a disembodied object, like a bubble or cloud. Ask it to make its case to you.
- Listen to what it communicates and then return the thought to your mind's back burner. Consider what the thought communicated to you for only a moment, giving it a minimal amount of time.
- Allow the next thought to come forward.

Here's an example: let's say you are trying to meditate when the thought comes to your mind that you didn't shop for dinner. Ordinarily, you might think of a quick menu, the items you'll need, and when and where you'll buy them if they're not already in your kitchen. That might lead to remembering that you're almost out of gas and thinking that you'll have to stop to refuel before you can go to the grocery store.

Instead of allowing yourself to be distracted, try neutralizing the initial thought by simply acknowledging that you didn't plan dinner yet. Don't assign any blame or judgment. Tell the thought: "I will plan dinner when my meditation is over." Give the thought your attention, assign it a place, and move on.

PROCESS YOUR EMOTIONS

Emotions are not amenable to logic the way the thought of planning dinner might be. Feelings may come through the body as sensations, pleasant or unpleasant. They may also appear as attitudes, especially toward yourself. For example, as you begin to sit in meditation, you feel restless, saying to yourself, "Okay, let's get down to business." What does this mean?

Initially, you may feel a wave of impatience because you procrastinated throughout the day and that procrastination is weighing on you. Then you may feel a wave of frustration as you're reminded that there doesn't seem to be enough time to do everything you want to do. Finally, a sense of anger may well up because the interference of others has taken up so much of your time.

Instead of giving in to these emotions, address the impatience with humor. "What's the hurry?" you might say. "I'm here to get *away* from business." Likewise, meet the frustration with calm, reminding yourself, "The time I give myself will multiply the time I can give to everything else." And always neutralize anger with kindness: "I have been inconvenienced by the interference of others, but now I can make it up to myself." Other feelings may appear when you begin to meditate: hopelessness, discouragement, and other counterproductive feelings. What would you say to a close friend who expressed those feelings to you? You would undoubtedly extend words of hope, encouragement, and motivation. Treat yourself the same way.

Your goal is to balance and settle your emotions. This is not a quick, easy task. You will need much practice, because you are probably harder on yourself than on anyone else. One attitude to always keep throughout this process is what the Dalai Lama, Tibet's spiritual leader, calls "loving kindness," meaning tender affection. Practice it on yourself as often as you can.

METTA (LOVING-KINDNESS) MEDITATION

Metta meditation is considered priceless; it is a treasure we can use to help create intimacy with ourselves and others. The Buddha was precise about the benefits of this meditation and proclaimed that:

- You will sleep easily.
- You will wake easily.
- You will have pleasant dreams.
- People will love you.
- Devas (celestial beings) and animals will love you.
- Devas will protect you.
- Poisons, weapons, and fire (external dangers) will not harm you.
- Your face will be radiant.
- Your mind will be serene.
- You will die unconfused.
- You will be reborn in happy realms.

To begin, come to a quiet place and breathe slowly until you begin to feel calm.

1. State this wish for yourself: "May I be happy and free from suffering." As you say these words to yourself, acknowledge all your goodness.

2. Next, think of someone you have strong respect and gratitude for, and visualize him or her as you state this wish: "May Jonathan be happy and free from suffering."
3. Next, think of a close friend and say: "May Paula be happy and free from suffering."
4. Next, think of a neutral person, someone whom you do not know very well (perhaps someone who works as a delivery person), and state: "May my mail carrier be happy and free from suffering."
5. Next, think of a difficult person, someone whom you do not like, and state: "May Harold be happy and free from suffering." This can be challenging. Maybe bring that person to mind and linger for a while, thinking about others whom you also do not like.
6. End the metta meditation by thinking of all beings, and state: "May all beings be happy and free from suffering."

Do not force or even try to manufacture disingenuous feelings of any kind, such as feelings of love for someone whom you do not like. Just say the words as though the words were delicate glass sculptures. In doing so, you may feel more loving toward that person and toward all beings.

DELVE DEEPER INTO THOUGHTS AND FEELINGS

Thoughts and feelings can take turns coming to the forefront during your sessions. If you feel comfortable acknowledging them and returning to your meditation, you may do so. If you find that particular thoughts and emotions refuse to be put aside, it might be time to spend some time examining them more closely. Asking questions is a beneficial exercise in noticing thoughts and feelings through meditation. This is not a process of analyzing. Rather, it is a way of exercising mindfulness, one of the qualities sought in meditation. Throughout the process, you are also bringing forth another innate ability: insight. Together, these dormant tools can provide you with honest, clear answers to all the questions you may have about yourself and your life in general.

When intrusive thoughts or feelings arise, spend a few minutes asking yourself the following questions:

- Why do I think/feel this way about that person or situation?
- What causes led to this thought/feeling?
- Why do I still think/feel this way about that person or situation?
- What conditions could make this thought/feeling change?

This is an exercise in "mental housecleaning." Like regular housecleaning, you can observe yourself doing it: layers of awareness unfold like the proverbial lotus, and you experience insights along the way.

As you become more adept at acknowledging your thoughts and emotions, an interesting phenomenon begins to happen. The rush of thoughts and feelings subsides, and you begin to notice that something else is present: your own awareness, anticipating the next thought or feeling. At that moment, there is a pause in thought and feeling, and it is that pause you are seeking to cultivate. That is meditation.

FORM AN INTENTION

Otherwise known as creative visualization, forming an intention for the day (or part of the day) can help guide your mind down the right path.

1. Set a timer for 5 minutes. Do some deep breathing and allow your mind to reflect on the particular course of action you would like to achieve. Picture plans falling into place, such as coworkers helping you achieve your goals and the complete cooperation of people and circumstances. Put all your mental energy into believing in this ideal vision. Note any resistance or skepticism.

2. When the timer goes off, say a brief prayer for the realization of this vision. When you open your eyes, make a plan on paper for your intention and stick to the plan as much as possible. You will be surprised by the results.

DISMISS THOUGHTS

Sometimes you find yourself inundated by negative thoughts. When that happens, try this calming meditation. It allows you to acknowledge your thoughts and then dismiss them, freeing up space for positive thoughts to enter your mind.

1. Sit in your meditation space, either in a straight-backed chair or cross-legged on the floor. Close your eyes and begin breathing deeply: eight counts in, hold four counts, eight counts out, hold four counts. Keep counting your breaths for four to six cycles. When you can maintain the same rhythm, let go of the counting.
2. Watch your thoughts. As they arise, dismiss them, silently saying "Not this" or "Not that." Keep your negation simple—don't attach any emotion or aggression to it. At the same time, keep your attitude expectant, as though you were waiting for something better than the thoughts your mind normally presents to you.
3. Continue dismissing your thoughts, one by one. Don't worry if you have trouble doing this—just keep trying. When you open your eyes, note any shifts in your perceptions.

RELEASE OLD WOUNDS

This meditation helps you release past hurts that may prevent you from expressing your full potential. You may have some traumatic experiences that have always lingered in the shadows because you were not capable of releasing them. These old wounds may make you overly cautious in some areas, or they may prevent you from developing emotional connections with others. As you go through this exercise, be gentle with yourself. Don't try to force yourself to let go of something before you are ready. Let your heart progress as it will. Deep breathing and visualization work will help. As you realize your own boundless power, the hurts of the past will seem less and less consequential. You may never forget what has happened to you in the past (and you probably shouldn't), but those past events will cease to have a strong hold on you.

1. Think about your heart. Feel your heart beating in your head, the rush of blood through your arteries and veins. See how the heart nourishes and enlivens your whole body. See it not only as an organ, but as the essence of yourself, spreading beneficial energy to your whole self: body, mind, and spirit.
2. Now ask your heart to reveal its wounds to you, the ways it has been hurt in the past that prevent your growth from going forward. Don't force the issue. If nothing comes to you, do not try to make the experience happen. You can always try again later.

3. Some scene from your past may appear in your mind's eye: a coworker who criticized you, a former lover who left you, a public embarrassment of some kind. Be prepared for something unexpected that you buried deep inside. Simply notice this wound from the past and acknowledge it. That may be as far as the exercise goes for now.
4. If you feel ready (and only if you feel ready), speak to that wound. Say to your past hurt, "I am ready to let you go. I forgive those who were responsible, I forgive myself, and I am ready to turn this wound into a source of strength." Picture the same radiant energy that pulses through your body washing over your wounded heart.
5. When you are finished with the exercise, your heart will still bear its wounds, but the scars will be healed to a greater degree than they were before. Particularly deep wounds may require multiple sessions.

EXERCISE GRATITUDE

Sit quietly and breathe in and out slowly until you quiet your mind and feel relaxed. Visualize, in as much detail as you are able, people whom you are grateful to have in your life: Begin with those you love, then extend your gratitude to anyone who has crossed your path in life and positively impacted you.

Visualize things you are grateful to have in your life: your senses, a blue sky, cool breezes, red wine, lobster, family, laughter, starry nights, full moons, vivid colors, music, washing machines, vacuums, fireplaces... whatever comes to mind.

Visualize qualities you have that you are grateful to have as part of your total being: persistence, dedication, cheerfulness, intelligence, and so on.

Bring your hands to a prayerful pose against your heart and offer thanks for your many blessings.

Once you begin to regularly exercise gratitude, you begin to vibrate gratitude. Done often, this can become an extremely rewarding habit.

CREATE GRAY SPACE

What does it mean to create gray space? One of the best ways to understand this concept is to think about childhood. When you were young,
you could sit and watch the pattern of raindrops as they cascaded down
a car window, or observe the pattern of lichen on a stone. You could lie
in bed on a Saturday morning and talk to yourself for hours, or take a
handful of sand and let it flow through your fingers. These in-between
moments are not exactly meditation, nor are they exactly intentional
actions. It's this type of gentle activity that is most vulnerable to being
edited out of our heavily scheduled adult lives.

Unwasting Your Wasted Time

When you live mindfully and incorporate meditation into your days,
you will notice that you have downtime when you don't have anything that
you are *supposed* to be doing. You will realize for the first time just how
much of your time was wasted before. Avoid the temptation to convert
these gains into more frenetic activity, or you will find yourself right back
where you started. Use at least half of this time to do nothing at all. Don't
even meditate. Instead, create gray spaces that are not meditating, not
daydreaming, not really anything. Allow yourself to go into a kind of mental hibernation. Your mind needs this downtime in order to recuperate—it
is doing a lot of work behind the scenes when you least expect it.

TRY A MOUNTAIN MEDITATION #1

Being in the mountains is a unique experience. The clear air, fresh breezes, sweeping vistas, and abundant foliage all provide nourishment for the soul. Just the idea of being in the mountains also gives you the perfect place to perform a quick and powerful meditation.

1. Lie down outside, if possible; if not, lie down on a bed.
2. Close your eyes.
3. Breathe long, slow breaths.
4. Let your entire body surrender into the support of the earth.
5. Picture Mother Earth wrapping her arms around you with healing love.
6. Feel the gentle mountain breeze blow across your face and body.
7. Feel the coolness.
8. Stand up slowly and take a refreshing breath, drawing in the fresh mountain air.

TRY A MOUNTAIN MEDITATION #2

Lie down if possible; if not, sit comfortably and imagine you are lying in the middle of a mountain meadow filled with wildflowers. Smell the earth, the fragrant flowers, the wild grasses. Feel the warm sun on your body. Listen to the sounds of birds in the distance, the humming of insects, the sound of the breeze rustling the trees.

1. Imagine that a mountain stream is off in the distance and that you can hear the movement of water.
2. Imagine all your concerns, worries, hurts, and disappointments flowing down the stream like fallen leaves. Imagine them floating away. Each time a thought comes into your mind, let it flow down the stream. Let it go.
3. Become so still that all your senses are alive.
4. Listen to the quiet sound of a fawn chewing young, green, wild grasses.
5. Relax. Let go of all thought. Come to a place of peace and quiet.
6. When you feel calm at your center, stand up slowly and then take a short walk in your surroundings, reveling in the beauty around you.

ACCEPTING CRITICISM

Criticism has a role to play during the creative journey because it helps sharpen skills, leading to better results. If free expression is the entrée into the creative process, taking criticism is the next threshold that must be crossed. People who can say "yes" to constructive criticism are destined to become better people, whether or not they realize it themselves. Here is a quick exercise you can do to effectively deal with criticism:

1. Determine if your critic has all the information and that information is accurate and unbiased.
2. Ask (calmly) for further explanation.
3. Consider if there has been a misunderstanding.
4. Consider if the intent of the criticism is malicious and only meant to hurt or if it is indeed constructive.
5. If you need it, ask for a small break to calm down.
6. When you are ready, give the messenger of the criticism some thanks, even if it is only for him helping you to reflect on the situation.
7. Say your view of the situation kindly, but assertively.

If, once you get past your initial hurt, you realize that the criticism might contain something valuable for you, then spend a few minutes meditating on that new information and on what actions you can take to further your success on this matter. Meditation helps in this area because it de-centers the ego and allows you to think of the situation as happening *through* you, not *to* you.

HONOR YOUR INNER CHILD MEDITATION #1

Here's the first of two opportunities to visit your inner child. After you have reconnected with your inner child, then you can move on to honoring the person you have become. For this meditation, find a quiet place to sit and close your eyes.

1. Breathe slowly until you begin to feel calm. (Never worry if you are not able to get to a calm place. That will come with time and practice.)
2. Think back to when you were a child. Try to remember a time when you were not feeling acknowledged or loved. See if you can remember the circumstances and what led to those feelings. Try to see yourself as a child in the memory. Embody the memory by remembering little details, like what you were wearing, what time of year it was, or who else was present.
3. During this process, keep your breath long and even, returning focus to your breath as needed. If the memory is really difficult or painful, you can choose not to go there and try another memory instead.
4. With your eyes remaining closed, "look" into the eyes of the child—remember, that child was you—and visualize wrapping your arms around her and talking softly with her. If she is crying, let her continue to cry while you hold her. If you begin to cry, let the tears flow.

5. When you both feel more composed, gently ask your inner child to tell you why she feels left out or unloved. Listen intently, allowing her feelings to wash over you.
6. When the story feels complete, tell her you are sorry she felt this way in the past. Reassure her that you love her and want to make her happy.
7. Say farewell to her. After a moment of resting in silence, go back to focusing on your breath. Inhale memory...exhale acceptance and love.
8. Continue breathing until you feel reenergized.

HONOR YOUR INNER CHILD MEDITATION #2

Another meditation that can help you honor your inner child involves happy memories!

1. Breathe slowly in and out until you feel calm.
2. Think back to when you were a child, to a time when you were feeling good about yourself, to a time when you were happy.
3. Remember any details, like what you were wearing and who was with you. Why were you feeling so proud or joyful?
4. See yourself as that happy child. Move closer so you can be with her and share the happy moment.
5. Notice how it feels to re-experience childlike joy. Can you bring that feeling into your life right now?
6. Stay with this experience, breathing slowly in and out, until you feel very happy and ready to play!

EMPTY YOUR MIND

It might seem impossible to actually have an empty mind because thoughts are natural for us, and they will never completely stop. However, you can learn to tame your mind not to go running after every single thought. Most of us can feel victimized by our own crazy heads at one time or another. It does not occur to us that we can stop obsessive, crazy, or repetitive thinking.

If you sit in the early morning, you will probably hear some birds sing. Your mind will register that the birds are singing. Most of us, by habit, will then think, "Oh, the bird is singing." Then we might think, "That sounds beautiful." We might go even further and think, "That reminds me of my vacation in Florida where the tropical birds sounded so amazing and we had that wonderful fish for dinner..." And so on and so on. When you hear the bird, try to catch yourself before you go on a 5-minute journey down memory lane. Eventually you will hear the bird and think, "Oh, the bird is singing. That sounds beautiful." Then, later, you might think, "Oh, the bird is singing." Eventually, you will just hear the bird. Empty mind.

Each human moment can be broken down into three parts. First you have an occurrence (the bird singing). Then you have the recognition of the moment (the thought that the bird is singing). Then you have the judgment on the moment (that the singing is beautiful). Aim to stay in the first part of the moment. To stay in the first part of the moment is to truly live in the moment. It is to experience the world as it really is and not as you have been taught to experience it. It is to be a part of the moment, completely and wholly a part of the moment. When you judge the moment, you remove yourself from it.

DO SOMETHING YOU LIKE

Create a ritual that nourishes you, something you can do every day even if you can only find 5 minutes for your ritual. It could be pruning flowers in your garden, enjoying a glass of lemonade while sitting in your backyard, going online to find a recipe you're dying to try, or calling your mother, best friend, or partner. Maybe you can find a quiet nook where you can light a candle and sit and write in your journal. Or maybe you'd prefer blasting a song from when you were in high school and dancing like a maniac. It could be absolutely anything that pleases you, as long as your daily ritual reminds you that you need a little pampering too.

GROUND YOURSELF

Try this creative visualization to help feel centered and grounded: write or think of an affirming statement, something like "I see myself creatively parenting my children to the best of my ability, offering guidance and love and patiently accepting whatever crosses my path." Relax with a few deep breaths. Feel the tension of the afternoon melt away like an ice cube in the sun. Feel yourself fill with an abundance of love and acceptance.

Visualize an area of life that makes you feel insecure. Visualize warm rays of sun shining on the parts of your life that you feel are in need of strengthening. Perhaps you desire more patience, for example. Let the rays of sun turn into a giant ball of healing energy; imagine this energy surrounding you. Allow any thoughts, fears, and emotions to rise up. Don't be afraid of them. Let them rise up, look at them with compassion, and then let them float away down an imaginary stream. Take another few breaths. Feel the lightness of letting go.

Continue your day feeling renewed and confident.

TAKE A TIME-OUT

If things are not going well and you feel yourself moments away from blowing a gasket, you need a time-out to calm the hurricane building inside. Forward-bending postures will calm the nervous system. Try this short, simple exercise:

1. Stand with your feet hip-width apart and your arms at your sides. Press your weight across the balls and arches of your feet. Soften your knees so they are slightly bent.
2. Reach your arms up above your head and inhale, then exhale. As you exhale, fold over to touch your toes or reach close to them. Hang like a rag doll. Your head should not have any tension. Stay for a few breaths.
3. You can sway back and forth, sweeping your fingertips side to side. Come up slowly, rolling one vertebra over the other like you are stacking coins. Your head should come up last.

You can do this as many times as you would like to feel calm and refreshed.

MANAGE STRESS WITH *SHAVASANA*

Shavasana, or the Corpse Pose, is a posture designed to help keep the body under control so that it doesn't interfere with the pursuit of meditation. And *shavasana* does just that—it helps rein in the body and get it working the way it is meant to work. For that very reason, *shavasana* is an excellent stress management technique.

Many yoga teachers consider *shavasana* to be the most important of all yoga *asanas*, or postures. *Shavasana* is both easy and challenging because all you do is lie on your back and relax, but...you actually have to lie on your back and relax!

To practice *shavasana*, find a comfortable spot on the floor. A bed usually isn't supportive enough, but you can lie on a mat.

1. Lie on your back with your legs about 2 feet apart and flat on the floor and with your arms flat and away from your body, palms facing up. Let your feet fall to the side.
2. Now, begin to relax as you breathe in and out through your nose. As you breathe, concentrate on fully relaxing your body: your bones, joints, muscles, everything. Let everything sink comfortably down toward the floor. Don't worry about how you look or what you should be doing. Just let it all go. Relax deeply. Stay in this position for 5 minutes (you can eventually work up to 15 or 20 minutes).

This pose is great after a yoga routine or any other kind of work-out. It's also an energizing way to start the day and a relaxing way to end the day. Doing *shavasana* is like pushing a reset button: it lets your body reset itself, realign itself, reenergize itself, and reverse the stress response.

PERFORM A CALMING STRETCH

When your body is tense and feeling stressed, try this simple 5-minute stretch to clear your mind.

1. Lie down on the floor on your back.
2. Bend your knees and place the soles of your feet on the floor. Your arms are by your sides.
3. Inhale, reaching your arms up and over your head. Rest them, palms up, on the floor above your head.
4. Exhale, bringing your knees toward your chest.
5. Inhale, reaching your feet up toward the ceiling and flexing your feet (toes toward your forehead).
6. Exhale, bringing your knees back toward your chest.
7. Inhale, bringing the soles of your feet back to the floor, using your abdominal muscles to control the movement.
8. Exhale, bringing your arms back to the floor beside you.
9. Inhale, lifting your hips upward a few inches.
10. Exhale, bringing your hips back down.

Repeat this simple stretch as many times as you would like.

MEDITATE ON MEMORIES

If you are having trouble sleeping, it often helps to focus on past memories, particularly ones that tap into times when you felt safe, happy, and loved. Here's how:

1. Lie down or sit on your bed (whatever is comfortable) and try to remember a time when you were particularly happy. Perhaps it was during your last vacation by the sea when you rented a cottage by the shore.
2. Pause for a few breaths, giving yourself time to remember. If memories don't immediately spring to mind, think about specific details such as your favorite part of the cottage (the tiny but comfy kitchen or the screened-in porch).
3. Close your eyes and think back to those happy days, and then try to see the cottage in your imagination: see the cozy room where you slept, hear the sound of the waves coming to shore, remember the taste of the salty sea. Pause for a few breaths to form pictures in your mind.
4. Try to draw yourself deeper into the meditation by attempting to remember the weather: Was it hot? Was it cloudy? Did it rain all week? Do you remember how it smelled after the rain? Do you remember how the clouds were bigger than you'd ever seen? How you saw angels and sea horses and sailing ships in the clouds?

5. Encourage more happy memories by remembering how the sand felt on your feet and how it squished between your toes. Do you remember how much fun it was to feel the waves? How the ocean was cold and the sand was warm?
6. Slow your breathing down and whisper "Hhhoooommme" ("home") as you exhale, replicating the sound of the ocean waves as they come to shore.
7. Keep breathing slowly in and out, saying "Hhhoooommme" (this is called *ujjayi* or *ocean breath*) as you exhale. Soon you will be so relaxed that you will drift blissfully off to sleep.

CALM YOUR NERVES WITH SEATED-FORWARD BEND

If your back is tight, here is way to ease your tension in just 5 minutes or less. Forward-bending postures like this will calm the nerves while also stretching leg and spine muscles.

1. Sit down on the floor with your legs extended.
2. Inhale; then, as you exhale, reach your hands toward your feet, hinging at the hips.
3. Let your arms relax by your legs and stay folded over with your head and neck relaxed.

EXPERIENCE *UJJAYI* BREATH

Ujjayi breath is a very calming breath that sounds like the ocean or the sound you hear when you put your ear next to a seashell. To achieve this breath, softly draw out the word *home* as you exhale: "hhhoooom-mme." Say this word in a whisper. Now say it again, but this time round your lips and gently close your mouth. You can also reverse your breath and draw in the word. It may sound like Darth Vader, but *ujjayi* breath is much softer and less scary. *Ujjayi* breathing has several benefits:

- It improves concentration while doing yoga and allows you to take full, deep breaths.
- It diminishes distractions and allows you to be self-aware and grounded.
- It regulates the heating of your body. The friction of the air passing through the lungs and throat generates internal body heat.
- It helps release tension in tight areas of the body.
- It can help sooth headaches, sinus pressure, and decrease phlegm.

SEND YOUR LIGHT MEDITATION

When life gets tough for your friends and loved ones, you can send them your love through this light-sending meditation. Send this love and light to all the corners of the earth. Know that your love is boundless, without borders or prejudice.

1. Sit in a comfortable seated pose, cross-legged if you are able. Or sit on a chair with your feet flat on the ground.
2. Bring your hands together and vigorously rub them until you feel lots of heat.
3. Place your heated hands over your heart center. Your heart center is in the center of your sternum, over your heart. Put one hand over the other.
4. Imagine the heat going into your heart and lighting a candle. Consider that when you go into a very dark room, just one candle can bring light.
5. Bring all your awareness to the heat and light at your heart center. Consider this heat and light to be all the love you have.
6. Send beams of this light/love in the direction of your loved one. As you send love, your heart becomes bigger and bigger and brighter with love and light.
7. Send beams of light to other family and friends, and to your colleagues. Send more light and love to neighbors, even those whom you do not necessarily like. Send them more light and love.

8. Next, send love and light to those whom you may see daily but do not really know: the barista who makes your coffee every morning at the coffee shop, your mail carrier, the school crossing guard.
9. Let this light in your heart become a giant ball of love and energy. Send this giant ball of light and love to your community, to your town, your state, your country, the world.

TRY *HAKALAU*

Are you looking for instant relaxation? Focusing on your peripheral vision can be deeply relaxing. The kahuna (shamen of Hawaii) called this technique *hakalau*, which means "to focus in and spread awareness." Here is how to use this technique:

1. Sit comfortably and relax.
2. Pick a spot in front of you and relax your eyes, blurring your vision just slightly.
3. Then, without moving your eyes, focus for a few minutes on what you can see in your peripheral vision.

STOP PESSIMISTIC THOUGHTS

You can use a fun behavioral technique called "thought stopping" to nip your pessimistic tendencies (and any other mental stress reactions) in the bud. To practice thought stopping, think of a negative thought you tend to have. Associate the thought with a clear image. Set a timer for a few minutes, close your eyes, and concentrate on the image. When the timer rings, shout "Stop!" Repeat several times. Then, whenever the image recurs, whisper "Stop." The interruption will stop the thought and give you the opportunity to consciously substitute the negative thought with a more positive one.

SAY WHAT YOU THINK

In the name of courtesy, people often don't say what they are thinking. Often, that's a good thing, but sometimes not expressing your feelings causes them to build up inside, increasing your feelings of stress. Sometimes it's just fine to speak your mind. If you are in the habit of holding your tongue, take 5 minutes out of your day and practice verbalizing what you feel more often, even if you just say the words out loud with no one else in the room.

MEDITATE ON WATER

If you are near a river, lake, or ocean, water meditation is an ideal way to feel at one with your surroundings. Humans are, after all, composed of up to 75 percent water!

Lie down and for 5 minutes consider your relationship with water. Our bodies are mostly water. The chemistry of the water in your body is like the chemistry of the salt water in the ocean. Do you feel the pull of the moon the way the tides do?

TRY A WATER MEDITATION

Walk around and see if you can feel watery: move as if you have no bones, feel as if you were fluid. Walk to a place where you can lie down, then lie down and close your eyes. Consider the healing properties of water, letting the water wash away all your concerns. Breathe, relax, and say the following:

"Rivers of tears, sometimes pouring out of me; at other times, just a trickle. Salty tears.

"Tributaries of capillaries nourishing every single part of my body. The flowing blood in my veins and arteries bringing oxygen to every part of my body.

"All the systems of my body...flowing."

LIVE MINDFULLY

Mindfulness is not confined to meditation—after developing this skill as much as possible, you will carry mindful awareness within you. It's applied to everything you do, from eating and working to learning and relaxing. The experiences in each day, from the insignificant to the momentous, become rich and vibrant when you meet them with mindfulness. For most, it's not possible to engage mindfulness at every single moment of the day. But the practice is rewarding, and there will come a time when it becomes the way you live your life.

It's as easy as slowing down your morning routine and performing each step with intention and focus, as though every single thing you do is the most important thing you have to do in your life. If you're new to mindfulness, it helps to focus on your breath for a few minutes and use that focus to quiet your mind. Then, you gather your senses and bring your full consciousness to what you are doing. Physically slow down, paying attention to sensory input (such as the feel of your clothing as it glides over your skin or the sound of the water running when you brush your teeth). If your mind wanders, always go back to focusing on your breath. This may feel awkward at first, but what you want to avoid is habitually (and unconsciously) rushing through these activities.

As you are brushing your teeth, for example, try not to think of your next activity. Instead, bring all your attention to what's happening in that moment: the feel of the brush as you use it to massage your gums and clean your teeth, the way your mouth feels sparkling clean after you rinse. Isn't it great that you have teeth to brush? Smile at yourself in the mirror!

Mindfulness is about staying focused on what's happening right here, right now, avoiding thoughts of the past or future. In the preceding example, just breathe and brush...breathe and brush. Mindfulness is also about savoring experiences and feeling gratitude for your blessings.

MEDITATION ON HOW TO EXPECT THE UNEXPECTED

Change is hard and can cause you to feel all kinds of emotions. Meditation can bring a sense of ease. No matter where you are, you can always bring focus to your inner body. You can choose to still your thoughts. You can choose to go to your place of wisdom within. See what it has to say. The more you can calm yourself by focusing on breath and moment-to-moment experiences, the clearer your intuition will be.

When you get upset or anxious about something unexpected (like the weather), you have already lost sight of living in the moment. When that happens and you become more anxious, focus on slowing and calming your mind.

1. Sit or lie down.
2. Tune in to your breath. Your breath brings you back to the present moment.
3. Notice the quality of your breath: how it is cool as you inhale and warm as you exhale.
4. Notice the feeling under your nostrils as your breath moves in and out.
5. Take a moment as you are focusing on your breath to notice how you are feeling. Disappointed? Anxious?
6. Do a body scan, from the top of your head to your toes.

7. Say each body part as you scan, noticing any sensations.
8. Notice if you have tightness in any parts of your body. Are you gripping within your body? Loosen your grip. Do you feel like you are losing control when the weather (or anything unexpected) changes your plans? Surrender your desire to control.
9. Notice your emotions. It is easy to have joy when everything is going the way you want—when it is always sunny during a summer vacation, it is easy to smile and be lighthearted. Being joyful is much more challenging when things do not work out according to plan.
10. Change can be uncomfortable. Notice where you feel it in your body: physically, emotionally, and/or mentally. When have you felt like this before? Take some time with this. Go back and remember when your body felt this way before.
11. Notice and bring yourself back to the present moment, to your breath.

PRACTICE *HARA* BREATH

Hara breath is a manner of breathing designed to relieve the body, mind, and spirit of stress and to reinforce a strong sense of self. *Hara* originates in the belly, which is your body's central region and the site of your soul power. *Hara* breath will give you an abundance of energy, speed your metabolism, and clear your mind to focus on the day ahead.

Focus on doing this by yourself, for yourself, but if others want to join you—and if you feel so inclined—welcome them into your circle. However, always stay focused on yourself so you can refill what feels depleted and thus have more energy to give later.

1. Stand with your feet slightly more than hip-width apart and your arms straight down by your sides.
2. Raise your arms up and squat down forcefully as you loudly say "Ha!"
3. Inhale, straighten your legs, and as you exhale, say "Ha!" with even more emphasis, emanating the sound from deep within your belly.

Repeat this up-and-down motion ten times (or as many times as you would like) and get ready to feel a burst of energy!

REBALANCE WITH TREE POSE

Tree Pose is perfect—physically and psychologically—for dealing with reentry stresses, such as going back to work on a Monday or readjusting to life after a vacation. It helps develop balance, steadiness, and poise.

1. Stand with your feet hip-width apart. Feel the four corners of each foot pressing evenly into the floor or ground. (This is a great meditation to do outside with bare feet, weather permitting.) Lengthen your spine and lift the crown of your head toward the ceiling (or toward the sky if you're practicing outside). Feel all the muscles wrapping around your legs. Gently engage your leg muscles, especially lifting the quad muscles. Lift your pelvic floor by pulling up your muscles (as though you were trying not to pee) and engage your abdomen by pulling the stomach muscles inward.

2. Bring the sole of your right foot to the inner thigh of your supporting left leg and open your right knee out to the side. (Feel free to touch a chair or wall to help with balance.) Bring your hands together in a prayer position. Look at something that is not moving to help with balance and focus on your breath until you feel steady. When you do, bring your hands up as though you were extending your branches.

3. While in Tree Pose, think about what tree you resonate with to-day. Are you a willow tree, swaying back and forth, or are you an oak tree, standing firm and strong? How about a cherry or apple tree?

If you are not able to balance today, use this as an opportunity to reflect on what may be out of balance in your life. As you do balancing postures, you may notice that some days you can balance for quite a while and other days not so much. Being mindful is noticing (without judging) the differences from day to day.

TURN EVERYDAY TASKS INTO MINDFULNESS MEDITATIONS

You can do anything mindfully—you can even clean a toilet mindfully! Become deliberate about the toilet. Go slowly and let the way you approach this task set the tone for the rest of the day. Choose a nicely scented and organic product. Pay attention to what you're doing instead of trying to rush through it. Notice the judgments you make about the toilet and about cleaning it. Notice how much time is wasted thinking about what you have to do instead of simply accepting that it must be done and attending to it. Part of meditation practice is acceptance. As you clean, focus on making the toilet clean. Think of it as a gift to your family. Imagine them noticing how delightful it feels to have a nicely scented and fresh toilet to sit down on.

Think about all necessary tasks as individual meditations. Washing dishes can be a perfect meditation! Fill up the sink with soapy water, again making sure to buy cleaning products that are beautifully scented and perhaps organic. When you plunge your hands into the soapy water, enjoy the sensation of warmth. Then, wash each glass and dish slowly, surrendering any desire to rush the process or focus on getting them all done. Focus on just one item at a time. Appreciate your dishware as you line up each item nicely in the dish rack to air-dry.

You can, with practice, make everything you do a mindful meditation, by quieting your mind, focusing solely on the task at hand, using all your senses, and breathing evenly, calmly, and slowly as you work. Enjoy the time by seeing it as a restful time, devoid of rushing or multitasking. Give yourself tranquility. For example, if the phone rings while you are doing your task, stop what you are doing, take a breath, dry your hands slowly, take another breath, and then answer the phone. Give all your attention to whomever is on the other end. When you are finished with your call, resume completing the task at hand.

VISUALIZE YOUR DESIRES WITH THE STIRRING THE POT MEDITATION

This meditation will help you visualize your heart's desire for your life by stirring the "pot" that is your body and mind.

1. Sit on the floor or a yoga mat. If it would feel more comfortable, place a folded blanket or small pillow under your hips. Cross your legs and bring your hands down onto your knees.
2. Pretend you are sitting on a big clock.
3. Lean over toward your right knee and circle your upper body toward your left knee. Continue circling around until you make a big circle going in a counterclockwise direction.
4. Inhale as you round forward, gently sticking out your chin.
5. Exhale as you round back, bringing your chin toward your chest.
6. As you are "stirring the pot," think back in your past. You are going counterclockwise! Think about something that hasn't worked out for you. Can you let this memory go?
7. Keep going around for a few minutes. What else comes up for you in your past?
8. Now reverse directions. This time, close your eyes and look up toward your third-eye point (the place between and above your eyebrows). Think about what you would like to see in your future.

9. As you continue rotating in a clockwise direction, pretend you have a great big canvas and that you are going to create a work of art. This work of art will embody what your heart's desire is. Take as long as you want creating this imaginary canvas. You can use imaginary paint, pen, photos, anything your creative imagination can come up with!

After you are finished creating a vision of your heart's desire, stop and "study" it with your eyes closed. What do you see?

When you feel ready, slowly open your eyes, retaining a clear memory of what your heart most wants to have happen.

DO SOMETHING SLOWLY

How many lists do we make in our lives? We often get ambitious and create a picture of how we want things to look instead of seeing how they actually are. If we learn to slow down our lives, though, things will become more relaxed and clear. When we are busy, we are focused on the future: what things could be, what we could have, or what we could or should do. We lose sight of the here and now.

Learning to go about daily chores mindfully can help you learn to slow down. Choose an everyday thing that you normally do, but this time, do it really slowly. This changes your focal point from "What is the next task/thing/sensation?" to the moment of concentration. It takes concentration to move slowly and mindfully, and that focus brings your attention to what is happening in the moment. To slow down is to honor each and every moment you have. You cannot count on your next breath, really. You only have the breath you are breathing.

As you slow down, you may begin to realize that your mind is always consumed by thoughts of the past or the future and is rarely in the moment. Doing things slowly brings your focus to the moment, making whatever you do a meditation. Slow moving creates (with practice) a calmer mind. Slow moving helps you notice the tiny details you usually miss.

TAKE A VIDEO VACATION

Don't have time to get away but want to feel the relaxation of a vacation? Take a virtual one! If you're at home, even if you only have 5 minutes, slide in your favorite DVD, sink your tired body onto some soft cushions, and let the story take your mind on a lovely side trip. This might work better if it's a story you already know well—that way, you won't feel compelled to watch to the end. If you know and love the story, you can pick and choose the portion you watch. You can choose a movie that sweeps you gleefully away, or you could watch nature videos. Choose whatever will leave you feeling refreshed and pampered. If you're at work and can take a short break, find something on the Internet you'd love to watch for a few minutes. Hint: you could also watch an exercise video, a yoga video, or a dance video.

FIND STILLNESS

Sitting in stillness is what meditation is all about. A meditation practice can be very challenging. It is hard to sit in stillness—our minds are chattering about all kinds of things all the time. This happens to all of us. This chattering mind is called "monkey mind," because like a monkey that jumps from branch to branch, our minds can seem to jump from thought to thought.

Ideally, meditation should be done every day during a time you set aside for just that reason. This can be very difficult for busy people, but we can all find times throughout the day to quiet our thoughts. As far as helpful breath (*pranayama*) and yoga postures (*asanas*) are concerned, the possibilities are endless. Take just 5 minutes out of your day today and sit in stillness, calm your monkey mind, and clear your thoughts.

RELEASE EXPECTATIONS

Are you one of those people who is always thinking about the future, often imagining that sometime in the future—when all your challenges have been successfully addressed—happiness will come? This way of being focused on the future often becomes an unconscious habit.

To counteract this tendency, pause for 5 minutes and sit quietly, or even lie down if possible. Breathe in and breathe out a few times, focusing solely on your breath. Quiet all mind chatter, then bring your mind to the present. Make a conscious decision to surrender the habit of focusing on the future. Choose to focus, instead, on what's happening right now, and choose to live more fully in the present. With your eyes closed, breathe in joy and peace...and then breathe out worry about the future. As you breathe, recognize that everything you need is already here, right now! Breathe in peace and joy...breathe out worrying about the future. The more you practice this meditation, the more you'll learn to focus on and live in the now. This is the foundation of real happiness.

TAP INTO YOUR INTUITION

Your intuition is related to the area of your third eye, which is located between your eyebrows. This area is considered to be a chakra (a swirling circle of energy) that is connected to your pineal gland, which is in turn located behind and above your pituitary gland, near the center of your brain. The pineal gland has characteristics like an eye: it has a lens and is sensitive to light. According to many ancient traditions, your third eye has special powers and is linked to a higher consciousness. You are able to stimulate this center of intuition in a few ways:

- Bring your hands together and press your thumbs firmly into the space between your eyebrows. Close your eyes and look up into that same space. Inhale and exhale deeply. After about 3 minutes, bring your hands down and keep your eyes closed. Thoughts, sensations, and even images may appear. Just notice what your third eye reveals. If you don't feel anything, be patient. Intuition takes time to develop.
- Slowly speaking the sound of "Om" will stimulate your third-eye chakra. Inhale deeply, and as you exhale, round your mouth slowly, allowing the sound to vibrate in your chest as you draw it out, saying "Ooooooooommmmmmmmm." The vibration will stimulate your third eye and open your center of intuition.

- Lie on your belly with your arms by your sides and your legs extended. Press your forehead (third-eye point) on the mat and just stay in this position for a while, or come to Child's Pose (on your hands and knees, resting your hips on your heels) and press your forehead onto the mat. If this bothers your neck, place your hands between your forehead and the mat, one on top of the other with your palms up, and rest your third eye on your palm.

Opening to the possibilities of intuition can bring you to a deeper connection with your spiritual body. If you do not practice a religion, consider opening to the possibility. If you do practice an organized religion, this third-eye opening can bring you to a deeper prayer life.

HONOR YOURSELF

Take 5 minutes today to honor the person you are. If possible, find a place to sit outside that faces the east (where the sun rises), or go to your sacred space inside and sit there. Light a candle. Acknowledge that the east is where each new day is born.

Reach your right arm and fingers toward the east and bring your left hand onto your left knee with your first finger and thumb touching. (The first finger represents your soul and the thumb represents the soul of the universe.) This is a mudra (a hand gesture) that symbolizes your connection to the universe.

Say:

- "I am the light of my soul."
- "I am bountiful."
- "I am beautiful."
- "I am bliss."
- "I am, I am."

Say each of these affirmations a few times out loud.

PART 2
CALM YOUR BODY

AWAKEN YOUR BODY

Let your day begin with a few nourishing moments by pausing to meditate. An awakening meditation is an opportunity to ground yourself and create intentions for how you want your day to go, which can positively affect the way things actually do go.

Awakening meditations don't have to be complicated or take much time, but do incorporate breathing and stretching if you can. This simple breathing-in-and-out meditation includes positive affirmations to start off your day on the right foot.

1. Lie on your back with your arms at your sides in a relaxed manner, or, if you like, place them palms-down on your stomach so you can feel your breath entering and exiting your body.
2. Begin by stating your intention aloud: "Today is a new day with 24 new hours to live; thus I gratefully choose to begin my day with meditation."
3. Then, as you slowly inhale, breathe in this thought: *I vow to start each and every day with an open heart.*
4. Pause briefly; then, as you slowly exhale, breathe out this thought: *I vow to accept with compassion what comes my way.*
5. Repeat this meditation four or five times.

FIGHT DEHYDRATION AND STRESS

Sometimes, one of the most helpful things you can do for your body when you're feeling anxious is to have a drink of water. Human bodies are about two-thirds water, but many people are mildly dehydrated and don't know it. While severe dehydration has dramatic symptoms and can even result in death, mild dehydration may go unnoticed and is more likely to occur after intense exercise, in extreme heat, while dieting, and after vomiting or diarrhea, either from illness or as a result of food poisoning or drinking too much alcohol.

Are you dehydrated? Symptoms of dehydration include the following:

- Dry mouth
- Dizziness
- Light-headedness
- Dark urine (should be pale yellow)
- Inability to concentrate
- Confusion

One reason people tend to be so often dehydrated is that caffeinated beverages are so popular and widely available. Caffeine acts as a diuretic to flush water out of your system. The other reason for dehydration is simple: people don't drink enough water anymore. Yet, water can offer your body many benefits, not the least of which is a stronger defense against stress.

Work More Water Into Your Life

Drinking more water is one of the easiest changes you can make to help manage your stress. Ideally, you should drink 64 ounces (or 8 cups) of water each day. If you space out your consumption throughout the day, it's very doable. Have 16 ounces first thing in the morning, 16 ounces with lunch, 16 ounces with dinner, and 16 ounces in the evening. Add another 16 ounces or more if you've been sweating or getting a lot of exercise.

If you really don't like the taste of plain water, try a few brands of mineral-added bottled water. The minerals give the water more flavor. Or add a wedge of lemon, lime, or orange to your water. If you just have to have those bubbles, try club soda instead of soda. Still not charmed? Dilute fresh fruit juice with water or club soda.

TOAST YOURSELF WITH A DRINK

If making dinner seems like a drudgery and is something that robs you of happiness, then why not add a bit of fun to the task. If you enjoy red wine, go ahead and pour yourself a glass. Just be sure to take a minute to mindfully notice the experience by savoring the taste, enjoying the deliciousness, and appreciating the luxury (even if it's an inexpensive wine!). Wine spritzers that call for mixing wine with soda water are also fun. If you're making Mexican food, why not have a margarita or a mojito? Don't get sloshed—that's never a good idea. The idea is to enjoy the time you're spending in the kitchen and to make dinner preparation an activity that brings you pleasure. If your partner is home, invite him or her into the kitchen to share a toast and help prepare the meal.

TAKE A MINDFUL SHOWER

Whether you shower before breakfast or after dinner, taking a shower provides a few minutes for you to focus on yourself. To take a mindful shower, first clear your mind of any distractions, then move slowly, enjoying each sensation as it occurs. If it helps, state your intention clearly aloud: "I am shedding all my worries to focus on my body and my senses."

1. Begin by stepping into the shower. How does it feel to go from dry to totally wet? Are the physical sensations pleasant or unpleasant? Stand still for a few minutes, letting the water run over you, quieting all thoughts, experiencing the rejuvenating powers of water.

2. Turn your attention to your feelings. How does it feel to have peace and quiet? Breathe in relaxation...breathe out frustration. Notice how worries dissipate and how good it feels when muscle tension subsides. Notice how unadulterated bliss feels in your body.

3. Notice all sensations, such as the fragrance in your soap or shampoo or the grainy texture of your face scrub. Allow the smells and textures to conjure up pleasant memories. Listen to the water as it cascades over your head and hair. What does it sound like? Listen as the drops of water strike the shower curtain or glass. How does it sound different from when it hits the

shower tiles? As steam fills the shower stall, does it make you want to draw swirls on the walls the way a small child would? Give it a try!

4. Dismiss all other thoughts. If thoughts about what will happen after your shower or what happened earlier come up, gently brush them aside. Stay focused on the sensations occurring in the shower. Stay fully present, living breath to breath, sensation to sensation.

5. As your shower nears its end, try humming. It not only feels good, but it can sound comforting to you and to your family if they can hear you. Feel the vibrations in your throat as you hum; attune yourself to this feeling. Often you can recall these sensations later and use them to supersede unkind words you may use throughout the day, particularly if you learn to associate kind words with the feeling of humming. Practice by saying kind words for yourself, such as: "May the words I use to describe myself be loving, kind, and nourishing." Then state an intention for the day ahead, such as: "May the words I use today as I talk with my coworkers/friends/family be full of love and kindness. May the conversations we share bring us closer together."

6. Toward the end of your shower, take a few really deep breaths, saying "Ahhhhhh" as you exhale.

7. Stay focused on sensations. When you get out of the shower, notice the texture of the towel you use to dry yourself. Notice

how it absorbs the water, how clean your dry skin feels against the towel.

8. As you look in the mirror, remember your promise to use kind, loving, and nourishing words when you speak about yourself (and others).

SAY GRACE

Even if you're not religious, saying grace at dinner is a marvelous way to express gratitude for all your many blessings and to teach your family to be thankful for the bounty before them. It needn't take long; a quick acknowledgment of the gift of food before you is all you need. You could create a ritual, such as lighting a candle, ringing a small bell, holding hands, or simply bowing heads to unify and focus the family on giving thanks. Each family member could have a special night to take charge of the dinnertime ritual, such as ringing the bell before offering grace. Welcome your children's spontaneous prayers (you can call them "intentions" if you prefer), as they're likely to come up with jewels. Make it okay to laugh—nothing relieves stress or bonds your family together like laughter.

TREAT YOUR SPINE RIGHT

Successful meditation does not depend on your ability to contort your body into the traditional lotus position of the yogi who sits cross-legged on the floor, but you do want to be sure your body is in a comfortable and anatomically correct position to ensure productive meditation.

When meditating, your spine should be upright and immobile. This position allows for optimum breathing and puts less strain on your body overall when you want to maintain one position over an extended period. Besides being a practice of proper breathing that aids circulation, the right posture ensures that your entire body can oxygenate and circulate blood without hindrance.

To be kind to your spine, you'll need to find the proper sitting posture for meditating. Sitting postures require a firm foundation, but at the same time, enough padding should be under you to promote circulation and comfort. Most easy chairs invite slouching and poor posture, but if you have a chair that allows you to sit upright comfortably, feel free to use it. If not, the floor is a good place to begin.

The second consideration is what to do with your limbs. If you are sitting on the floor, should your legs be crossed or folded? Should your feet be tucked under you or at your side? You'll need to do some experimentation here. Keep in mind that circulation is more important than how your position looks. If you plan to sit in a chair, the same guidelines apply. However, your feet must be supported, either by the floor, a footrest, or a cushion.

For 5 minutes, try sitting in several different positions. If within that time you start to feel numbness in your feet, legs, knees, or bottom, get up and move around. Then try another sitting position. Do this until you find a position that is comfortable and relaxing. You can now go to this position anytime you need to feel relaxed.

UNDO STRESS WITH A TENNIS BALL MEDITATION

This exercise will help you release those knots of stress you may be keeping in your back. Find a tennis ball that is used and just a little flat. Keep this tennis ball handy as you begin.

1. Turn on a mindless TV show and lie down on a rug or yoga mat.
2. Use your right hand to place the tennis ball under your back, between your spine and your left shoulder blade.
3. Bend your left knee, bringing your foot up close to your bottom.
4. Inhale, releasing your hands down by your sides.
5. Exhale, letting the weight of your body slowly come down onto the tennis ball.
6. Press into your left foot to roll your back a few inches up and down over the ball. Notice the valley of knots! The tennis ball is staying on the left side of the spine.
7. Find your most tender knot and allow your body to sink onto the ball. Say (or moan) "Ohhhhh."
8. Breathe deeply. If this is too intense, put a towel between you and the tennis ball. If you want to intensify this exercise, straighten your bent leg.
9. Do the other side.

TRY TWISTING POSE

This spinal twist will loosen your midsection and neck. Remember to keep your breathing slow and steady while you do this pose.

1. Sit up tall on a chair or bench. Sitting at the edge will help lengthen your spine. Bring your chin slightly toward your chest to lengthen the back of your neck.
2. Inhale deeply, then exhale, saying "Haaaa" and letting your breath fall away. Repeat a few times.
3. Begin to breathe in and out of your nose, slowly and deeply.
4. Inhale. Then, as you exhale, bring your left hand over to your right knee, draping it around your knee (if comfortably possible).
5. Turn your head to gaze over your right shoulder.
6. Bring your right hand behind you and press down on the seat for leverage to help keep your spine erect.
7. Stay in this posture for a few minutes, then switch sides.

RELEASE TENSION WITH A BACKBEND

Here's another exercise that will help release tension in your back. It can be especially useful midway through a long day at the office.

1. Sit at the edge of a chair or bench.
2. Inhale through your nose, then exhale, saying "Haaaa." Repeat a few times.
3. Inhale and reach your arms forward, clasping your hands and inter-lacing your fingers.
4. With your fingers interlaced, turn your palms away from you.
5. Round your spine and bring your chin to your chest.
6. Exhale and reach upward, keeping your fingers interlaced. Look up (but do not crunch the back of your neck).
7. Arch your back. Think of your heart center reaching forward and lifting upward. In other words, you are arching more in the upper back than anywhere else.
8. Reach as far as you can. Stay in this posture for a couple of minutes.
9. Come forward again, rounding your spine.
10. Do this a few times. Always come slowly out of any backbend, rounding your spine to release any tension.

STIMULATE THE THROAT CHAKRA

The energy located in your throat chakra has to do with personal expression, which can often become blocked. Taking a moment to open it in the morning will help you express your true feelings—with full power and intention—throughout your day.

1. Sit on the side of your bed and inhale deeply.
2. As you exhale, stick out your tongue as far as you can and say "Ahhhhhh." Do this forcefully.
3. As you stick your tongue out, notice how the sound emerges. Notice that you can choose to make your words sound harsh or kind.

Sticking out your tongue will relax your throat and stimulate your throat chakra, reminding you about truth-telling. When your heart and throat chakras are stimulated, you cannot help but speak from a place of love and compassion. Sometimes the truth hurts, so take a moment to create an intention for your day, such as "May all the words I speak today be filled with love, compassion, and truth."

RELEASE FEAR WITH
A COBRA POSE MEDITATION

Cobra Pose is a great energizing pose for the middle of the day—the nature of the movements helps release whatever stress or fears have arisen and helps restore your energy. Here are the moves of Cobra Pose:

1. Lie on the floor facedown with the tops of your feet touching the floor. Spread your hands palms down on the floor next to your shoulders.
2. Press your thighs, the tops of your feet, and pelvis into the floor.
3. Breathe in and begin to stretch your arms, lifting your chest off the floor, keeping your elbows close to your sides and pointing behind you.
4. Engage your abs and draw your belly button toward your spine.
5. Continue lifting your chest, keeping your hands, hips, and feet firmly planted on the floor. Tilt your chin upward and lift your chest to the ceiling.

If you do Cobra Pose every midday, you will feel more energy and you will open possibilities for the second half of the day. This pose can be an antidote for depression. It also improves the flexibility of your spine, strengthens your back, facilitates deeper breathing, and releases tension. It can also help release fear, which tends to manifest itself in the lower back and can get "stuck" there. When you do back-bending postures like this one, you can use this simple meditation to help release fear:

1. While you are in Cobra Pose, allow any fear (past, future, or current) to surface. Take a few breaths to recognize the fear.
2. Inhale and think: *I am aware of fear from my past and my fear of the future.*
3. Exhale and think: *I breathe out all this fear.*
4. Then, close this meditation by affirming this aloud: "Fear no longer serves me."

LEARN TO EAT MINDFULLY

Eating too much weighs down your body and makes you feel sluggish. Overeating at night keeps your digestive system working overtime and can disturb your quality of sleep. Eating too many simple sugars can raise your insulin level and promote bingeing, which perpetuates the cycle of overeating. Eating too much can also, of course, cause you to become overweight.

Eat Slowly

Eating slowly is a meditation? Yes. With the busy pace of life these days, all too often we eat on the run or shove in food before our next activity. Slow down—your body and your mind will thank you! Invite family members to try this, too, to whatever degree they are able.

1. Make a place at your table and sit down to eat. Look at your food, pausing to breathe, noticing the smells, the textures, the colors. Even if it is a very simple and ordinary meal, you can savor the beauty and delight of your food. A plain bowl of oatmeal is a thing of beauty when you slow down and really look at it. Consider how it was created. How amazing is it that food emerges from the ground? Food actually grows!

2. Bow your head in gratitude for the food, pick up your fork or spoon, and take a bite. Let the food linger on your tongue for a few seconds before you begin to chew.

3. Chew slowly and for a long time. Really taste each bite. You may think something is bland at first, but then with further investigation, you might realize it's actually sweet. Eat your entire meal like this: slowly and mindfully.

IMPROVE DIGESTION WITH THREE-PART BREATH

As a gentle massage to your abdominal organs, this breath will improve digestion: when you inhale deeply, your diaphragm pushes on or massages your lower organs, stimulating your digestive tract.

1. Lie down on a rug or yoga mat. Bring one hand to your abdominal area and one hand to the center of your ribs.
2. This breathing is done with long, slow, deep breaths. Inhale first into your abdomen, letting it expand into your hand. While still inhaling, let your breath expand your rib cage and then expand your upper chest.
3. Exhale, letting your abdomen soften, your ribs come together, and your upper chest relax. Continue doing this three-part breath for 5 minutes.

STIMULATE DIGESTIVE DELIGHT

This yoga pose helps relieve constipation and improve digestion. It's a great pose to do before bed, particularly if you've eaten a heavy meal. (If you have a slipped or herniated disk, be very careful with or avoid this posture.)

1. Sit down on a rug or yoga mat and extend your legs. Bend your right knee and cross your right foot over your left leg. Your right knee is pointed upward; your right foot is on the mat near your left knee. Make sure your spine is lengthened and you are not slumping. Press evenly through your hips and buttocks so that you feel your weight evenly distributed. If your spine rounds, sit on a folded blanket to tilt your hips forward and help lengthen and straighten your spine.
2. As you slowly inhale, wrap your left arm around your right knee.
3. As you exhale, bring your right fingertips to the floor behind your hips and look over your right shoulder.
4. While maintaining the twist, breathe deeply in and out several times, then repeat the same motions on the other side.

EAT YOGURT

Indigestion is a common reaction to stress because the stress response signals the body to channel blood away from the digestive system. The next time you suffer from an attack of indigestion, rather than popping antacids on the run, try sitting still for 5 minutes, breathing deeply, and savoring a cup of unsweetened yogurt. The "friendly" bacteria in the yogurt may help promote healthy digestion.

START A FOOD DIARY

Often, stress is related to food consumption. Did you eat too much of something, did the foods you ate make you feel sluggish, did the food leave you feeling guilty? Taking just a few minutes each day to write down what you ate and drank and any food-related feelings or problems you encountered can be a real eye-opener and can show you some problems with your eating habits.

If you get in the habit of keeping a food diary, you'll be surprised at how obvious your bad habits become. You might notice that when you are feeling stressed or insecure, you eat sugar, whereas when you are feeling confident or calm, you eat really well.

The important thing is not to beat yourself up over these things but to notice your negative or unhealthy patterns and change them. Keep food journaling until you feel in control of your eating habits; later, if you start to slip again, go right back to journaling. You might want to also share your food journal with your doctor, nutritionist, or physical trainer (if you have one).

STRETCH AWAY TUMMY TROUBLES

This posture will stimulate your abdominal organs and digestive tract. If you do this every day, it can help restore and maintain digestive health. This posture also gently stretches your lower back and keeps your vertebrae aligned.

1. Lie on your back on a rug or yoga mat. Press your heels down, lengthening as you flex your feet, creating a nice stretch for your back and hamstrings. Inhale, bringing your breath down into your belly. As you exhale, bring your right knee up toward your chest.

2. Wrap your fingers around the front of your knee. Continue breathing deeply. As you inhale, release your knee slightly, and as you exhale, draw your knee firmly toward your chest, keeping your extended left foot flexed (toes pulled toward your forehead). Repeat a few times with your breath. This movement will massage the ascending colon. (Always start with the right knee, as this is the direction of movement in the colon.)

3. Reverse sides. Bring your left knee up toward your chest and wrap your fingers around your knee. Breathe deeply. As you inhale, slightly release the hold on your left knee, and as you exhale, draw the knee firmly toward your chest. This will stimulate the descending colon. Keep your extended right foot flexed. Repeat the cycle for several minutes.

4. When you are done with both sides, bring both your knees up toward your chest and wrap your arms around your knees. Give yourself a big hug and gently roll from side to side.

DISCOVER YOURSELF

To ask the question "Who am I?" is to open your heart to discovery. When you stop the hustle of your busy life and sit in quiet meditation, you may start to realize that you have no idea who you are. What does it mean to be tall? What does it mean to be a woman? What does it mean to be an accountant? Does a tall, female accountant capture the essence of who you are? What if you added other characteristics of who you are? Take a few minutes and write down ten characteristics that describe who you are.

Now take a look at the entire list. Do these adjectives capture you? For instance, you might have written down the following: male, short, thin, beard, funny, hiker, graphic artist, dog owner, food lover, and athe-ist. Is that all you are? Are you more or less than these words? Do these words, in fact, capture anything at all about you? I am sure the answer is an emphatic "No!" There is some "other-essence" about you that you cannot capture with words. This otherness is something elusive that you cannot put your finger on.

You are not a string of words, a group of adjectives and nouns. Even if you were a group of adjectives and nouns today, those adjectives and nouns might be different tomorrow. We are always changing, never the same from one moment to the next. On a simple level, even if you are a graphic artist today, you might not be a graphic artist tomorrow. Per-haps today your hair is brown, but tomorrow it will be blond. Scientific research shows that seven years from now, not one cell in our body will be the same as it is today. Tomorrow you won't even physically be the same "you" as you are right at this moment. Your skin, hair, your very cells will be different.

The simple fact is that you are ever-changing and cannot be tied down to a particular idea or word. So why hold onto them? You are more than words. People cling so tightly to their labels, but learning to release them will help you let go of your fears and open you up to new discoveries.

JUST SIT

Zazen is the sitting meditation of Zen Buddhism, but many so-called Zennists who don't practice Buddhism do practice *zazen*. *Zazen* can be defined as "just sitting." It doesn't require any religious or philosophical affiliation—all it requires is the ability to apply the seat of your pants to the floor and stay there for a while. Sounds easy, you say? Hardly.

For those of us accustomed to accomplishing something every moment of every day, just sitting is quite a challenge. But just sitting accomplishes amazing things if it is practiced regularly. The mind becomes calmer. The muscles stay more relaxed. Stress fails to get the rise out of your body and your mind that it once did. Suddenly, priorities seem clearer; truths about life, people, and yourself seem more obvious; and things that used to stress you out hardly seem worth consideration anymore.

1. To begin, sit cross-legged or on folded legs (sitting on your feet), with a firm pillow under your hips so that you aren't sitting directly on your legs. Make sure you are wearing enough clothes to stay warm. Sit up straight, feeling a lift from the crown of your head toward the ceiling and an open feeling in your spine. Keep your shoulders back and your chest open. Place your tongue on the roof of your mouth.
2. Focus on a point that is slightly downward and relax your eyes.

3. Now, unfocus your eyes just a little so that you don't really see what's in front of you. This will help you focus inward.
4. Rest your hands in your lap. Keep your mouth closed and breathe through your nose. At first, practice concentrating by counting each breath. In your mind, count from one to ten, with each full breath (inhalation and exhalation) constituting one number. Or simply follow your breath, keeping your awareness focused on the sound and feel of your breath moving in and out of your body.

ROAR LIKE A LION

If you have pent-up feelings that you need to release for you to move on, mimicking a roaring lion should do the trick. This pose relaxes your face and neck, which helps release a clenched jaw.

1. Sit on your heels, bring your hands onto your knees, open your fingers like the claws of a lion, and lean forward.
2. Open your mouth as wide as you can, stick out your tongue as far as you can, and open your eyes as wide as you can.
3. Inhale; then, as you exhale, roar as long and as loud as you can. Keep roaring until all the bad feelings have dissipated.

REALIGN WITH PELVIC TILT

Your midsection can get very cramped if you sit for long periods of time during the day. Try this pose to realign your body.

1. Stand with your feet slightly more than hip-width apart, keeping your knees slightly bent. Inhale and bring your hands to your knees.
2. Exhale as you round your spine, bringing your chin to your chest. Tilt the bottom of your pelvis forward.
3. Inhale as you reverse this position: arch your back, look up, and stick your chest out.
4. Continue tilting and arching for about 5 minutes.

TRY CRANE POSE WITH GOLDFISH

Crane Pose with goldfish is a balancing posture that is perfect to do with kids. Use goldfish crackers for this activity (choose an organic whole-wheat version, if you prefer).

1. Stand on a rug or yoga mat and place a few goldfish toward one end of each rug or mat. (Kids love to have their own mat to use.) Stand in Mountain Pose. In Mountain Pose, your feet are hip-width apart, with toes facing forward. Bring your arms to your sides. Allow your tailbone to reach downward as you lengthen your spine upward. Press out through the crown of your head.

2. Now you are ready to begin the Crane Pose. Reach your right arm up over your head and make a crane beak with your fingers and thumb. Press your four fingers together to create the upper part of the "beak" and use your thumb to make the bottom of the "beak."

3. Bring your left foot to your left hand (behind you) so that you are balancing on your right leg. When you feel balanced, your crane face can look for the fish and decide to go fishing for a snack. Try to fold at the hip as you reach down to see if your crane can pick up the fish without you letting go of your left foot. Go slowly and steadily. When you have the fish in your "beak," come back

up while still balancing on one foot. It's fun to pretend that the crane is eating; it's even more fun to pop the fish into your own mouth.

With children, it is important to let them play with this exercise. They will pick up posture and alignment in time. Try to maintain your alignment so they can see how it looks. Kids will usually fall a lot while trying this, which is fine—it becomes part of their play.

TAKE A BREATH OF JOY

This pose will actually bring a smile to your face!

1. Stand with your feet about 1 foot apart, with your knees softly bent.
2. Inhale as you raise your arms in front of you to shoulder height...
   inhale some more, opening your arms out to the sides...inhale even
   more, raising your arms overhead...and then exhale, saying "Ha!"
   as you swing your arms down toward the ground, bending forward
   from the hips.
3. Use momentum to swing your arms back up to shoulder height as
   you bring your body upright. Repeat as many times as you like.
4. Keep going and begin to pick up the speed. Make each "Ha!"
   louder than the previous one. You will find yourself smiling and
   maybe even laughing!

LET LOOSE WITH ANIMAL YOGA

Pretend to be an animal! Start with Downward-Facing Dog Pose:

1. Come to your hands and knees on a rug or yoga mat. Curl your toes under, spread your fingers wide, and press your hips upward. Press into your hands as though you were pushing yourself away from the top of the mat. Pull your shoulder blades down, straighten your legs, and press your heels downward.
2. Come to your hands and knees. Make sure your hands are under your shoulders and your knees are under your hips. Inhale as you lift your tailbone and the crown of your head, looking upward. Let your lower back arch downward. Pretend that your heart is a flashlight beaming light directly in front of you.
3. When you exhale, tuck your tailbone under, round your spine upward, and lower your head. Do one execution while pretending you are an angry Halloween cat. Go back and forth between dog and cat, making sure you connect your breath to the movement.

BUILD CONFIDENCE WITH WARRIOR POSE

A true warrior has strength and wisdom and a strong heart. A warrior celebrates another's victory with generosity. It's not about who wins; it's about being strong enough to compete with honor and both win and lose gracefully. It's about honoring your opponents and yourself—win, lose, or draw. Here is the Warrior Pose:

1. Start with your feet hip-width apart.
2. Inhale and place your hands on your hips.
3. Exhale, step your left foot back, bend your right knee, and allow your body to sink down through your hips and buttocks. Press back through the heel of your left foot.
4. Inhale and raise your arms upward, bringing them perpendicular to the floor and parallel to one another. Reach your arms as high as you can to stretch your rib cage. While continuing to breathe, hold this pose for 30 to 60 seconds.
5. To release, lean forward and bring your left foot back to meet the right. Bring your hands back to your hips.
6. Take a few breaths, then do the other side.

RELEASE SHOULDER TENSION MEDITATION

Tension can build in your shoulders just as it can in your back. If you're feeling weighed down—whether literally after you've carried groceries or metaphorically due to emotional burdens—try this tension-releasing meditation.

1. Comfortably sit on the floor, using a folded blanket or towel for cushioning.
2. Inhale for a count of five; exhale for a count of seven. Your breath is creating space. You are not able to bring new things into your life until you let some things go.
3. Stay with this breathing until you are feeling calm (or at least calmer than before).
4. Have the intention of letting some things go.
5. With your eyes closed, notice how you are feeling in your physical body. Notice if you feel tension in your shoulders. Do you hold the weight of the world on your shoulders?
6. With your eyes closed, think about who or what is on your shoulders and causing you to feel weighed down. You may have your entire family lined up on your shoulders. Picture all of them lined up. What else or who else is there? Friends, aging parents, work responsibilities? Take time to really notice all the people and "stuff" you are carrying.

7. Inhale into your belly.
8. Exhale slowly; then, as you lean to your right, reach your right arm straight out and tilt over until your fingertips touch the floor.
9. Watch as everything and everyone slides off your shoulders, joyfully "listening" as they scream "Wheeeee!" while soaring down the slide that is your arm. Let them slide off, trusting that they will be fine, that they don't need to rest on your shoulders.
10. Inhale into your belly.
11. Exhale slowly. Repeat the same motion with your left arm, letting everything and everyone on that side slide off. You may have to shake your arm, as some people will (consciously or unconsciously) hold on really tight, even if everyone (especially you) knows it's good to let go.
12. You have created space by making your exhale longer than your inhale. You have also let quite a few things go. You can now fill up with calm, peace, joy, or whatever you need.
13. When you have fully exhaled, you have given all you can. Nothing remains except to have faith in your next inhale.

TENSE AND RELEASE

If your day has come to an end but you are still feeling wired, you can try to tense and release. Begin by paying attention to your breathing. Is it fast or slow? Close your eyes and breathe slowly in and out, drawing your breath into your tummy and then slowly blowing out all the air. Then follow these steps:

1. Lie down on your bed, straighten your legs, and lay your arms by your sides. Tense or curl your toes under, inhale, and then relax your toes as you exhale.
2. Tense your feet by pretending you are pointing your toes toward your forehead and pushing your heels away from you. Inhale while your feet are tense; as you exhale, relax them.
3. Tense or squeeze your buttocks while you also tense your legs, feet, and toes. Inhale. As you exhale, release your buttocks, legs, feet, and toes.
4. Pull your stomach in tight, until your rib cage is sticking out. Bring your shoulders up to your ears. Inhale. As you exhale, relax your tummy and shoulders.
5. Clench your arms and your hands (making a tight fist), lifting them about 1 or 2 inches off the bed. Inhale. As you exhale, relax your arms and hands, gently dropping them back on the bed.

6. Close your eyes and mouth really tight. Inhale. As you exhale, relax your face.
7. Clench your entire body, including your buttocks and face. Inhale. Hold this for a few seconds. Then, as you exhale, say a really long "Ahhhhhhhh."

DO SOME MINDFUL LAUNDRY

We have so much in our lives, so much to do and so much to follow up on, that we end up ignoring a great deal of it. We mindlessly do a simple task, such as laundry, with no consideration for the abundance that fills our lives. Every household chore you do can be an opportunity for mindfulness. Stay in the moment, and be thankful for the task at hand. Pay attention to your hands and the rest of your body as you move through the house. Be mindful of the noises you hear and the scents that greet you. Focus on what you are doing, and every time your thoughts start to wander, bring them back to the task at hand.

Doing laundry is an opportunity to be thankful, to be in the moment, and to realize the connection we have with all things. When you put the bag of laundry down by the washing machine, say a mindful intention before you begin. For example, be thankful for the clothes that protect you from the elements. Say aloud, "I am thankful for these clothes. These clothes protect me and keep me safe and help me maintain my well-being. I am thankful for the fabric from which these clothes were made, and for the hands that worked the machines that stitched the seams together."

Be mindful of your greater connection to the world as you touch the clothing that covered your body this week. Be grateful for the means to keep your clothing clean and fresh. As you separate the clothing, be mindful of the colors, the variety, and the feeling of the fabrics in your hands. Fill the machines and marvel at the abundance of water you have at your fingertips, but be careful not to waste water by using a larger cycle than is necessary.

CLEANSE YOUR ENERGY

If you've been around people whose negative energy has rubbed off on you, take an energy-cleansing "shower"!

1. Stand and imagine you have removed your clothing. Inhale and reach your arms up.
2. Exhale and lower your arms to your sides, imagining a shower of sparkling gold light trickling over your body.
3. Repeat the motion several times, allowing the gold light to cascade over your body and wash away all the negative energy you may be feeling or may have picked up during the day. Visualize the negative energy flowing away from you and being absorbed by the earth.

TRY WALKING MEDITATION

In Zen, walking meditation (*kinhin*) is the counterpart to sitting meditation (*zazen*). *Kinhin* is meditation on the move. Walking meditation is different from sitting meditation because you have to be thinking about what you're doing so that you don't wander into traffic or bump into a tree. On the other hand, it isn't really so different, because in sitting meditation, you become acutely aware of your surroundings.

Walking meditation is an excellent alternative to sitting meditation. Some people like to sit for most of their meditation session but then spend the last few minutes in walking meditation; for those who practice sitting meditation for longer periods of time, walking meditation gets the body moving periodically without breaking the meditative flow.

- You can do walking meditation outside or around a room. Either way, you should have a prepared path in mind so that you don't spend time thinking about where to go during the meditation. Begin by spending a moment focusing and breathing to center and prepare yourself.
- Then—taking slow, deliberate steps—walk. As you walk, notice how your breath feels. Notice how your limbs move, how your feet feel, how your hands and arms hang, the position of your torso, your neck, your head.

- Once you feel you've fully observed yourself, begin to observe the environment around you as you walk, but don't let it engage you. If you catch your mind wandering, gently bring your thoughts back to your breathing.
- Walk for 5 minutes. If you enjoy this practice, add 2 minutes every week until you're up to 15 to 30 minutes of daily walking meditation.

TREAT YOUR LEGS RIGHT

Not only is putting your legs up the wall great for circulation, it will also calm you when you are agitated and stressed—perfect for an evening stress-relief session. It takes so little effort and is surprisingly relaxing.

1. Find a quiet place in your home, bringing a small blanket and pillow with you.
2. Begin by sitting up straight with your hip against the wall.
3. Bend your knees and swivel around until you get your legs up the wall. Your buttocks should be touching the wall. Your body and legs should form a right angle.
4. Once you are in position, to achieve the natural curve of your back, lift your hips and put the pillow under them, nestling it into the small of your back. You want a gentle lift of your hips, with your tailbone spilling over the pillow toward the wall. You may want to put a small folded blanket or rolled towel behind your neck to lengthen your neck and allow your chin to be at the same height as your forehead. This pose should feel comfortable and natural.
5. When you are settled into the pose, you can begin the meditation, bringing physical, emotional, mental, and spiritual awareness. Here's how:

- Scan your physical body, from the crown of your head to your toes. First, bring your awareness to the top of your head and notice every sensation there. From there, bring awareness to your face and all the muscles around your eyes, jaw, neck, shoulders, and arms, going all the way to your fingertips. Work your way slowly down the back and front of your body—chest, belly, pelvic floor—always resting for a few breaths in each body part and acknowledging any feeling that may be present. Work your way down from your hips, legs, and knees to your ankles, feet, and toes. As you do this, imagine that your body is divided in half. Notice just the right side, then the left. Take a moment to reflect on the differences you feel in each body part.
- Next, move to your emotional body. Notice any emotions that may be present. Are you anxious about the coming week? Are you still happy after meeting your friends for a quick brunch? Is there a feeling you've been reluctant to acknowledge, even to yourself? Really take the time to look at each emotion and bring awareness to it.
- Scan your mental body. Notice thoughts, images, chatter, or whatever is present at the moment. Your mental body may be very busy, even mid-meditation. Just notice what kind of chattering is going on. Are you making lists, planning, going over a past conversation, reliving a past experience? Don't linger on any one thought too long. Just notice and be aware.

- Finally, bring awareness to your spiritual body. Does your spirit feel light or burdened? Do you feel any connection to your spirit? To a spiritual force of the universe? Don't make any judgments; just notice.

6. Visualize letting all of this go with your exhale. Inhale and feel your breath filling your lungs...exhale everything out. Repeat. Give yourself a few minutes to continue to "watch" your breath. With every exhale, let something go. You may be letting go of a tight hip or a feeling of sadness. Once you feel that a lot has been let go, just enjoy the sensation of your breath. Stay as long as you are able.

7. When you are ready, bend your knees and roll to one side. Stay there for a few breaths, press yourself up and stay seated for a few breaths. When you are ready, come to a standing position, wrap your arms around yourself, and give yourself a hug.

TAME EMOTIONS WITH FISH POSE

If you wake up feeling upset or angry, Fish Pose will help you tame your emotions, regain your center, and come from a place of love...which is naturally your intention.

1. Lie down on a rug or yoga mat and straighten your legs, flexing your toes upward. Extend your arms alongside your body.
2. With palms upward, roll from side to side as you take hold of the fleshy part of your upper back legs. Press into your elbows to bend them and use them to lift your chest upward. Let your head drop back (notice that your heart and throat chakras are open). You may want the top of your head to touch the floor lightly. Keep your legs strong and pressing downward.
3. Breathe slowly and deeply through your nose. Visualize your breath going into your heart and your throat and swirling around. Stay in the pose for five breath cycles or as long as you like.
4. While in the pose, consciously work on releasing emotions. Let the emotions flood outward. Let this pose be a moving meditation. Breathing in, think: *I am opening my heart.* Breathing out, think: *I am aware of my emotions.*

This is called Fish Pose because it resembles a fish: a fish is flexible and strong, capable of moving through water with ease. If you need more flexibility in your life—and who doesn't?—Fish Pose is a great way to start.

TAKE A BREAK WITH STANDING COBRA

This posture is great for an office break.

1. Face the wall and place your hands at shoulder height, pressing them against the wall. Spread your fingers, feeling them press into the wall, and bring your elbows close to your rib cage.
2. Slowly lean forward, leaning until your body is pressed against the wall and your forehead is resting on the wall. When you press your forehead onto the wall, you will be stimulating the third eye. Stay here for a few breaths with your eyes closed.
3. Inhale and press firmly into your hips. Exhale, lift your heart center as though you want to press it up toward the ceiling, and arch your back, letting your head reach back, opening your throat, and lengthening from your hips all the way up the front of your body. Think about the arch being in the upper back and not the lower back. Keep your neck long and not crunched. Stay for a few breaths.
4. Bring your forehead back to the wall on the exhale. Do this "wall cobra" a few times.

LET GO WITH LYING-DOWN COBRA

This is a longer version of the standard Cobra Pose that will help you focus on your breath more and uncover some things that have been troubling your mind.

1. Start by lying on your belly on a rug or yoga mat. Begin with your head turned to one side and your arms relaxed by your sides. Settle your hips by rolling slightly to your right side, rolling your left thigh inward, and then rolling slightly to the left side, rolling your right thigh inward. Pause briefly to rest.

2. While resting, practice push-up breath. As you inhale, allow your breath to go deep into your belly, expanding your belly until it presses into the mat. As you exhale, let your belly pull inward. Exaggerate this breath to create a feeling of the belly doing push-ups. This is a good exercise to remind you to breathe deeply into your belly in all meditative situations. Do this push-up breath for a few minutes.

3. When you are ready, bring your forehead to the mat. The area just between your eyebrows and about an inch up is called your third eye and is considered to be a place of intuition. As your forehead rests on the mat, consider whether or not you trust your intuition. How often have you had a feeling about something or someone and were right about that feeling in retrospect?

4. When you are ready to move into full Cobra Pose, place your hands (with palms down) directly under your shoulders. Your shoulders should be pressing away from your ears and down your back. Pretend you are holding a grapefruit with your shoulder blades and keep your neck long.

5. With your eyes closed, "look up" to where your third eye is located. This looking up will stimulate your sense of intuition, thereby deepening your meditation.

6. Lift up from the crown of your head as you press into your palms and raise your upper body a few inches. See how this feels. If you feel that you can raise yourself higher, keep slowly straightening your arms. If you are strong enough, completely straightening your arms and allowing your bones to support your upper-body weight offers an intense stretch for your back. If it feels too stressful, you can try placing a rolled-up blanket under your pelvis to cushion your pubic and hip bones. If at any time you feel a slight pinch in your lower back, bend your elbows until the pinch goes away.

7. While your shoulders are down, notice how your heart center opens. To deepen your meditation, think of your heart as a flashlight beaming light on the wall in front of you. Imagine pressing your heart forward (this is more of an intention than an actual movement) to release love and light into the universe.

8. When you are in the full expression of the Cobra Pose, breathe in and out of your nose for about five breaths. As you inhale, think: *I am opening*. As you exhale, think: *I am letting go*.

9. If you are gasping for breath, then the stretch has become too intense—you need to lower your body until your breath flows more easily and evenly. Holding your breath is another indication that you are too deep into the stretch, because as with any yoga posture, if it is more than you can handle, you may automatically begin holding your breath. Remember: your breath should be flowing easily and naturally at all times. Pushing the stretch is not desirable. Proceed at your own pace, knowing that the more you practice these stretches, the more limber you will become.

10. After five breaths, lower yourself to the mat and turn your head to one side to rest. After a moment, you may enjoy releasing any muscle tension in your lower back by slowly "windshield-wiping" your feet and legs from side to side.

11. Before repeating the pose, while resting, come up with a mental list of things you can release to make your day go more smoothly. Is there something you are ready to let go of? Maybe a few of the items on your to-do list, for example? Are there a few things you could say no to? Consider these things as you go into Cobra Pose again. As you keep opening into the posture, see yourself rising up to possibilities and challenges. Did you notice any fearful thoughts occurring when you first did the pose? Were you able to release them? If not, can you do so now, using your breath and focused intention?

RELAX WITH SPHINX POSE

This pose is very similar to Cobra Pose and has many of the same benefits as Cobra, but Sphinx Pose is much gentler.

1. Lie on your belly on a rug or yoga mat or press your body against a wall for a standing version.
2. Come up on your elbows, palms down, with your fingers pressing down and pointing straight ahead. Your legs are straight behind you and your thighs are rolled in; the fronts of your thighs are moving toward each other and the backs of your thighs are moving away from each other. Relax your buttocks and legs to open up your lower back. Feel your pelvis drop into the mat or press into the wall.
3. Close your eyes and take a few slow breaths. When you are done, bring your elbows out to the sides and bring your head to one side. Stay resting for a few more breaths.

VISUALIZE THE CAVE OF THE HEART

As you go along in your busy day, it can seem impossible to find a quiet moment anywhere. If you're feeling that way, try this meditation. It reminds you that you carry a shrine within you wherever you go: it's in the cave of your heart.

1. Sit up straight, either cross-legged on the floor or in a chair with your feet on the floor. Begin by breathing deeply, concentrating your awareness between your eyes. When you have entered fully into a rhythm of deep breathing, observe your internal space, the darkness before your eyes. You may see subtle lights, like electric sparks floating around. You may see mental formations, such as words and images, or you may see the outlines of your body or the room in which you are sitting.

2. Gradually move your center of awareness downward along your spinal column, going until your awareness rests in the center of your chest. This may be a little difficult, because many people think of the head as the seat of consciousness. With a bit of effort, though, you should be able to remain in the chest region. Now begin to see this space. You may sense darkness, or you may visualize your heart and lungs expanding and contracting.

3. Now allow this area to fill with a white light tinged with violet. Picture this light as a countervailing force against the words and

images in your head in the same way that the sun breaks through rain clouds after a storm. Make this inner vision stronger, concentrating until the light is extremely powerful.

4. After the visualization is established, stop trying to consciously produce it—instead, go back to simply observing. Realize that light and darkness are not opposites but are part and parcel of the same reality.

DO A BODY SCAN

The body scan is a popular relaxation technique that involves a mental scanning of the entire body in search of tension and the conscious release of that tension. You can do a body scan on your own, or you can have someone direct you by speaking out loud and naming the parts of your body, in order, so that you are cued when to relax what. You can also record a recitation of your own body scan cues and play it back for yourself.

The body scan is a great way to wind down after work or to calm down before a stressful event. Practiced every day, it can become a way to maintain a tension-free body and a body-aware mind.

Different people do the body scan in different ways. Some people like to tense each area of the body in turn, then fully relax it. Others prefer to visualize the release of tension without actually contracting the muscles first. You can imagine breathing into and out of each body part, exhaling away the tension one area at a time. Whichever way you choose is fine. You might try several ways to find which one you prefer.

PRACTICE YIN

You can use yin postures as an opportunity to investigate what's happening now—you can look at an emotion with curiosity, then let it go. Emotions are sometimes held in our bodies for years. Yoga postures and meditations can help release these stored emotions to bring a lightness to your overall being.

Yin yoga consists of passive postures that you hold for several minutes. The purpose of each posture is to get into the connective tissues of the body, to tug and tax the tissues to create suppleness. Most injuries that athletes and non-athletes experience are not injuries to the muscles—they're injuries to the joints. Fortunately, creating suppleness in the joints helps prevent these injuries. Yin postures work by relaxing muscles and strengthening and lubricating the connective tissues within joints. Once a joint is lubricated, it is less apt to be damaged.

Each yin posture stimulates a different set of meridians (energy channels) that run throughout the body and that stimulate and balance specific organ functions. Each organ is related to a particular emotion. As busy adults, we may become out of balance from all kinds of things: stress, exhaustion, multitasking, and so on. When we are out of balance in our kidneys, the emotional flavor is fear; the spleen, worry or obsession; the liver, anger; the lungs, sadness and grief; and the heart, depression and hatred.

Here is a simple yin position called the Star Pose:

1. Start in Mountain Pose (feet are hip-width apart, with toes facing forward, arms are at your sides), then step your feet wide apart, with your arms out to the sides. Your feet should be under your wrists, facing forward and parallel.
2. Press your weight into your feet, squeeze your thighs, tuck in your tailbone, and imagine your feet are strong and rooted to the floor.
3. Reach out through your fingertips, trying to touch the walls on either side of you. Relax your shoulders down and back.
4. Inhale and press the top of your head toward the ceiling. Look straight ahead and make sure your chin is parallel to the floor.
5. Inhale into your belly and then as you exhale press into your feet, fingers, and head, feeling your body expand in five directions.
6. Hold for four to six breaths.

REGROUP YOUR THOUGHTS WITH EYE CUPPING

Here's a quick, yet surprisingly effective meditation that can be done anytime you need to regroup.

1. Cup your hands over your eyes so that you cannot see any light. Close your eyes and feel the darkness for a few slow breaths.
2. While your hands are still cupped over your eyes, open your eyes slowly. This may feel very peaceful. Imagine that you are in the deep shade, in the middle of a forest. Invite peace into your little "cupped" space.
3. When you feel peace entering and feel reassured that you are ready to handle whatever comes next, remove your hands.

LOOSEN UP WITH RAG DOLL POSE

Rag Doll is a fun—and mindful—pose that would be great to do before you get into bed. This pose will teach you how to let everything go and focus on only one thing: total relaxation.

Stand up really straight, with your knees slightly bent (or "soft"). Bring your arms upward as you inhale; as you exhale, gently fold over just like a rag doll, allowing your arms, hands, and fingers to loosely hang down. It is not important to try to touch your toes—Rag Doll is about just hanging. Pretend you are a pair of pants folded over a hanger, then pretend you are a rag doll hanging over a railing. Visualize what the rag doll would look like. Imagine how a rag doll would breathe, what it would sound like. Inhale through your nose, then say "Ahhh-hhh" as you exhale through your mouth. Stay for a few breaths, inhaling through your nose and exhaling by saying "Ahhhh" through your mouth.

BREATHE AWAY THE STRESS RESPONSE

Many people are in the habit of shallow breathing, which is chest breathing. While this allows quicker respiration and is handy in emergencies, shallow breathing doesn't plumb the depths of the lungs the way deep breathing does. A few slow, truly deep breaths can stop a stress attack in its tracks. Deep breathing also helps you expel more air from your lungs, which is important for efficient lung functioning.

When told to breathe deeply, people tend to gulp in a huge amount of air with a dramatic uprising of the chest. Actually, deep breathing happens much deeper in the body—the stomach and abdomen should rise and fall, not the chest (and especially not the shoulders). The exhalation is the focus.

Breathing from deep within your torso is hard to do if you aren't used to doing it. You used to do it as an infant, but as an adult in a high-stress world, you may have forgotten how. The easiest way to retrain yourself to breathe deeply is to begin by lying down. Lie comfortably on your back and put one hand on your abdomen and the other on your chest, then do the following:

1. Begin by breathing normally. Be conscious of your breathing, but don't try to manipulate it.

2. Now, try to exhale every last bit of breath slowly, making an "sss" sound. When you think you've exhaled every bit of breath, give your lungs one more push and let out a final "sss" of air.
3. After this deep exhalation, you'll naturally take in a deep breath, but don't try to suck air into your chest—just let your body refill and take in air on its own. As your body refills, try to keep your chest and shoulders still.
4. Exhale again, slowly, as fully as possible.
5. Repeat for ten deep breaths.

Once you've mastered the feeling of deep breathing, you can try doing it sitting up. Again, focus on the exhalation. A good calming breathing exercise is to measure your breathing by silently counting, making the exhalation twice as long as the inhalation.

WIND DOWN WITH CHILD'S POSE

This is a great relaxing pose to include in your bedtime ritual. Begin by coming to your hands and knees on the floor or your bed.

1. Inhale; then, when you exhale, lower your hips down to rest on your heels.
2. Stretch your arms straight down by your sides, palms up, and keep your forehead gently resting on the floor or bed.
3. Try to make yourself really small—curl up even more.
4. Once you're in Child's Pose, you can gently roll from side to side, moving no more than 2 inches back and forth. You want your motion to be a soothing, rocking sensation.

CALM DOWN WITH COBBLER'S POSE

Another relaxing pose to try is Cobbler's Pose (also known as Butterfly Pose)—this pose helps you calm your mind and body.

1. Begin seated with your legs outstretched in front of you.
2. Bend your knees and bring the soles of your feet together as you let your knees fall to either side.
3. Draw your feet in as close to your body as is comfortable.
4. Sit up tall with a long spine and keep your shoulder blades down.
5. To make the pose more comfortable, you can put a pillow under each knee.

RELEASE TENSION WITH FOLD-OVER POSE

Many people tend to hold a lot of tension in their hips and shoulders, creating tightness in their lower backs. When you open your hips in this posture, it will also open your lower back.

1. In a sitting position, cross your right ankle over your left knee.
2. Feel both of your hip bones pressing down evenly.
3. Inhale, filling your lungs, then exhale, folding forward until you feel your right hip and buttocks release and open up. Place your arms on the inside of your right calf, folding one palm over the other. Let your back relax into the fold. You want to be at an edge, meaning that you want to feel this strongly but not painfully. The point that occurs just before pain begins is a good strong edge.
4. Once you feel your edge, commit to staying still for 3 to 5 minutes. During this long hold, try to relax all your muscles, letting the tug happen deep inside your joints. Breathe evenly. If you are holding your breath or gasping, you are too deep into the stretch and need to back off. If you are confident in your ability to do this pose and do not feel that you need to monitor your breath, close your eyes and become aware of all your physical, emotional, and mental sensations.
5. Do not judge what may come up for you. Just notice with curiosity, then let the sensation go.
6. After a few minutes, switch sides.

SIP YOUR WAY TO CALM

Here's a quickie breathing exercise that will rev up your energy. Many people do not breathe fully—they have old breath swirling in their lungs, because they only use about a quarter of their lung capacity. When you fully exhale, you create space to bring new and fresh breath (*prana*) into the lungs. This full breath will release serotonin and create a feeling of peace.

1. Pretend you are breathing through a straw and inhale little sips of breath without exhaling. Sip in as much breath as you can. Fill all five lobes of your lungs with breath until you cannot sip any-more...then exhale out of your mouth.
2. After you've exhaled and you think you are done exhaling, exhale some more. This kind of breathing is so very energizing that it should not be done in the early evening, because it will keep you awake.

REJUVENATE WITH COUCH POSE

Find one fun thing to do before the day ends. It could be anything, no matter how silly. How about a yoga pose that will amuse you and give you a badly needed energy boost?

Couch Pose is a supported shoulder stand that's a great rejuvenator. It gives your heart a break from constantly pumping blood all the way down your legs and back up again, and it also helps blood rush into your upper body and face.

Please note that you should not do inverted poses if you have high blood pressure or problems with your eyes. Even if those conditions don't apply to you, when doing this pose, always make sure that your neck is fully supported (you can place a folded blanket or pillow under your shoulders) and always heed any pain: if it hurts, don't do it!

1. Grab a folded blanket or soft pillow and place it on the floor in front of your couch.
2. Sit on the couch directly above the blanket, then swivel your body and swing your legs up onto the back of the couch with your legs straight.
3. Shimmy your hips to the very edge of the couch. Raise your hands up and over your head to steady yourself as you slowly lower your head and shoulders toward the floor. Pause to position the folded blanket or pillow under your shoulders, then

slither down until you are resting your head on the floor. Your shoulders and neck should be softly curved and feel fully supported by the folded blanket, while your hips are supported by the edge of the couch.

4. When you feel completely supported, position your arms overhead as if they were goalposts, with your elbows softly bent and your palms facing up.

5. Stay upside down, breathing, for as long as the pose feels comfortable.

You will feel marvelous after you come out of this Couch Pose.

SQUEEZE IN A 1-MINUTE MEDITATION

You can still meditate, even if you have just 1 minute!

1. Stand with your feet hip-width apart (each foot should be directly under its respective hip) and your knees slightly bent (this is also known as "soft knees" because they're not rigid the way they would be when standing normally). Bring your hands onto your thighs. Inhale and arch your back, gazing upward, sticking your buttocks out.
2. Quickly exhale and round your back, tucking your tailbone in and bringing your chin toward your chest. As you move, breathe in and out of your nose forcefully, executing this move quickly. You could do this seven times in just 30 seconds.
3. For the second half of the minute, stand up tall and notice how you feel filled with energy. Breathing in, think: *I have moved my body*. Breathing out, think: *I am energized*. Repeat this several times, then resume breathing normally.

RELEASE WORRY WITH
STRAIGHT-LEG FORWARD BEND

This pose is also good for the kidneys and for releasing worry.

1. Sit up straight on the edge of your chair or bench.
2. Take a few breaths. Inhale through the nose, then exhale, saying "Haaaa."
3. Breathe deeply through your nose (or through your mouth if that's more comfortable).
4. Straighten your legs in front of you and flex your feet by pressing your toes toward your forehead. Feel your hamstrings stretch.
5. Lean forward without bending your knees. Come to your edge—that point just before pain begins—and stay there for a few minutes.
6. You can stay with this stretch while watching your surroundings. If you don't need to monitor what's around you, try closing your eyes.

Notice any physical, emotional, or mental experiences you may be having, such as a tight hamstring or feeling overwhelmed or worrying about something happening in your workplace. Each time a thought or emotion surfaces, try to replace it with a breath. Or you can envision a stream and picture each thought or sensation or emotion as a leaf floating by. For example, you may be in your posture and realize that you are planning dinner in your head. Look at this thought…and then let it float by. You may be in a posture and begin reliving a quarrel you had with a family member. Notice this and think, *Rather than attaching to this quarrel, I'm going to let it float down the river.* This leaf-floating of sensations and thoughts becomes a mindfulness meditation. Some people also picture troubling thoughts or emotions as butterflies that flit easily away into the breeze.

TAKE A LUXURIOUS SHOWER

Taking a shower—or bath—provides a few minutes for you to focus on yourself. Choose your favorite scented soap (or bath oil or gel), shampoo, and protein treatment for your hair, then revel in bringing your attention to what's happening in the moment. Breathe deeply and pause to feel the soothing oil as it skims over your skin, the warmth of the water as it rushes over your body, and the soothing pulses of the showerhead as the water warms your neck muscles. Instead of rushing, gently massage your scalp and temples as you apply the shampoo and protein treatment, massage your neck or hands, or give your feet a hard scrub. Do whatever feels like pampering, taking the time to luxuriate in each sensual moment.

HUG YOUR KNEES

In addition to stimulating your heart and lungs, this pose is great for digestion, as it gives your lower organs a gentle massage.

1. Sit upright, bring your knees toward your chest, and wrap your arms around your knees. Keep your shoulders and chin down.
2. Your feet should be up off the ground—you'll be balancing on your bottom.
3. As you inhale, let your belly press into your quads; as you exhale, bring your navel in toward your spine. Stay for a few minutes, just focusing on your breath.
4. Once you've returned to a sitting position, briefly bring to mind any worries or problems or emotions that may be tying up your digestive process, then quickly and consciously release them.

GOING WITH GRAVITY

Being pulled in a dozen different directions by people, work, and responsibilities can take a toll on you, both physically and mentally. This meditation reminds you to reconnect with the natural forces that are in play around you all the time.

1. Find a place where you can lie flat on the floor without being disturbed. Turn off the light (if you can). If you feel any discomfort, place a cushion beneath the small of your back, behind your knees, and/or under your neck.
2. Set a timer for 5 minutes. Practice deep, slow breathing. Become conscious of gravity pulling your body into the floor. Imagine gravity pulling any tension out of your body and pulling away disturbing thoughts as well. Become one with the floor beneath you; imagine yourself to be an inanimate part of the floor.
3. Allow yourself to rest in a state as close to mindlessness as you can achieve. When the timer sounds, try to take some of this interior silence with you.

APPRECIATE YOUR BODY

Next time you get out of the shower or bath, take a few moments to notice your beauty. Look in the mirror and promise to use kind, loving, and nourishing words when you speak about yourself (and others). Notice the blush in your skin, the color of your eyes...really notice. If you look closely, there may be little dancing flecks of blue or gold in your eyes. Admire your beauty and feel grateful for your blessings.

Show appreciation for your body. Use your favorite lotion (with a little sweet almond oil added in, if you have some) to gently massage your body. Massage your feet, your legs, your belly, your arms, your throat, your face, and finally, your hands. Say a prayer of thankfulness for your body.

JUST DANCE

Whether you take an organized dance class—ballet, jazz, tap, ballroom dancing, swing dancing, country dancing, square dancing, Irish dancing, to name a few—or go out dancing with your friends, dancing is great cardiovascular exercise and also a lot of fun. Something about music makes exercise seem less like exercise, and dancing for fun (even alone in your house with the music blaring) is about as "unexercise-like" as you can get, yet it still comes with all the benefits of exercise. Vigorous dancing can also be an excellent way to relieve tension and anxiety, so get up and shake it!

MEDITATE WITH YOUR HANDS

Some consider mudras to be meditation in your hands. That's worth a shot the next time you have a stressed-out moment! Mudra refers to an ancient, sacred positioning of your fingers, used by Buddhists to guide the flow of energy during meditation. The ancient Buddhists believed that curling, stretching, crossing, and touching various fingers allowed you to wordlessly communicate with body and mind. Far more recently, the National Academy of Sciences found that hand gestures can activate the same regions of the brain as those activated by spoken or written words. The *prithvi* mudra, created by touching the tips of your ring fingers to the tips of your thumbs during meditation (while extending and relaxing all the other fingers), helps promote a sense of stability and increases tolerance and patience, which can prove beneficial when you are stressed. Take 5 minutes now and practice the *prithvi* mudra.

HINDER HEADACHES

A nasty tension headache can ruin your whole day and make everything you do more stressful. As soon as you feel a tension headache coming on, try running hot water (not uncomfortably hot) over your hands for 5 minutes. This process will draw blood away from your head and into your hands, which could stop a tension headache in its tracks.

TAKE A *ZAZEN* BREAK AT WORK

Even if you work in a cubicle, you can practice *zazen* right at your desk. *Zazen* is the sitting meditation of Zen Buddhism. If you are feeling stressed out at work a *zazen* break can help you. You can take *zazen* breaks in almost any profession. If you have a 5-minute break, do some breathing exercises to rejuvenate your flagging spirit and release some tension.

1. Sit up straight and focus on your breathing. If you are uncomfortable closing your eyes, keep them open and focus on the floor.
2. As you breathe in, watch the breath as it comes into your nose, down your throat, and into your lungs, expanding them. Imagine the breath going down through your stomach into your *hara*.
3. Then imagine the breath coming back up your stomach, out your throat and nose, and into the world. Follow the breath all the way to the end, and you will find a blankness there. The stress will seep out of you if you do these exercises for several minutes.
4. Try to continue the exercise until you feel the stress abate somewhat and until your thinking slows down.

Sometimes your thoughts can start to race at work as you get caught up in the drama of the day. Learn to space breaks so that you interrupt this cycle of thinking and avoid becoming wholly ego-driven. At the end of the day, it is not work that exhausts you—it is incessant thinking. It drains you and wears you out.

TRY REFLEXOLOGY

You can perform reflexology on yourself! Here's one to try.

1. To stimulate your brain when you really need to think clearly, hold up one thumb, then squeeze the tip with the thumb and index finger of your opposite hand.
2. Squeeze the middle of your thumb's tip, then make little squeezes in seven slow circles around the tip of your thumb, never fully releasing pressure.
3. Repeat on your other thumb.

SLOW DOWN ON SUNDAY

Even if you sneak in some rest on the weekend, by Sunday afternoon, the demands of the coming week are beginning to weigh on you. By nightfall, you can feel completely overwhelmed by the challenges of a week that hasn't even begun yet.

Don't give in to tomorrow's worries today—Sunday is still a day of rest. Rather than hurling yourself headlong into the next week, relax into it with a special Sunday meditation. This meditation doesn't have to be anything formal or intricate—just sitting in your favorite place with a cup of hot coffee and mindfully savoring the taste, smell, and appearance of it (watch how that luxurious cream swirls around in the cup!) or even just simply sitting somewhere quietly and noticing your breath are all quick and easy ways to regroup for your week ahead.

Put your weekly planner aside and embrace this perfect opportunity to rest, revitalize, and renew. These 5 minutes—you do have 5 minutes for yourself!—will help you set your intention to remain serene in the face of stress, no matter what the days ahead may bring.

BREATHE PROPERLY

Most of us breathe too quickly and too shallowly. To learn to breathe more slowly:

1. Breathe in to the count of five, pulling air into your lungs and into your solar plexus, allowing your belly to swell.
2. Pause briefly, then breathe out to the count of five, allowing all the air to slowly expel, allowing your belly to sink.

Breathing in from your diaphragm (rather than your lungs) will help you learn how to deepen your breathing. It's also helpful to place a hand on your belly so you can feel it rise and fall as you draw in and expel slow, deep breaths. Practice proper breathing for just 5 minutes a day, and you will notice you feel more relaxed and calm.

GET TO SLEEP

It's easier to fall asleep when your body is relaxed. Naturally, this is difficult to achieve when you are worried and tense, but a simple 5-minute muscle-toning exercise can help. Be sure to maintain conscious breathing when doing a sleep meditation, because good oxygenation will induce a relaxed state and encourage yawning—always a good precursor to sleep.

1. Lie on your back with your hands on your stomach, your legs extended, and your eyes half closed. Avoid curling your body into a ball or lying on your side.
2. Gradually focus on your body, beginning at the feet. Focus your attention only on your bodywork. Starting with the feet, turn them inward and curl your toes downward as tightly as possible. As you do this, inhale. Release slowly while exhaling. Move to your calves: turn them inward and tighten the muscles while inhaling. Release slowly while exhaling. Now focus on your thighs, tightening the muscles while inhaling. Release slowly while exhaling. Move your attention to the torso. As you inhale, allow your stomach to expand fully. Slowly exhale.
3. Tense and then release your hands while inhaling and exhaling. Do the same with your arms and hands while simultaneously raising your shoulders upward toward your ears. Inhale and

exhale while tensing and releasing. Tense your head by raising your chin upward as far as possible while inhaling. Slowly release it downward while exhaling. Avoid twisting your neck to the right or left.

4. Finally, perform three conscious breaths while wriggling your fingers and toes.

ANTICIPATE THE GOOD IN TOMORROW

Bedtime is an ideal time for meditation. Begin with something really simple, such as focusing on breath. See if you can hear your breath. Try to breathe noisily for a few times. Next breathe really quietly, breathe into your belly and blow out all the air. Breathe again and again. Breathing this way and focusing on your breath will naturally clear your mind and help you feel calm.

When you are relaxed, think about what you would like to have happen the next day. Choose one activity or event that you are eager to experience, then visualize the event as if it is already happening. Concentrate on where the event would take place, who would be there, how each person would behave, and how you would feel when everything goes exactly as planned—or better. When you have completed your visualization, it's time to close your eyes and drift off to dreamland, where you can revisit your pleasant visualization.

KEEP IT SIMPLE WITH AN IN-OUT MEDITATION

This meditation is simple, traditional, and great to do right before you get into bed for the night.

1. Begin by sitting in a comfortable seated posture on your floor, rug, or yoga mat.
2. Lift your hips up a tiny bit so that your knees are in alignment with your hips. If needed, place a small pillow or a rolled towel under your hips.
3. Lengthen your spine and bring your chin toward your chest so that the crown of your head is reaching upward.
4. As you slowly breathe in, say "In."
5. As you slowly breathe out, say "Out."

That's it. Seems simple, and it is. But simple does not mean easy! As your mind wanders, gently but firmly bring it back to focusing solely on the in-out breath. Replace your thoughts with your breath. Stay for 3 minutes to start, then work your way up to 5 or more minutes. Learning to quiet your mind and focus on your breath is key to mindfulness. You may enjoy this place of "nonthinking" so much that you will want to remain in this meditation for longer periods of time.

When you are ready to come out of the meditation, open your eyes, breathe normally for a few breaths, and go to bed.

PREPARE FOR A PEACEFUL SLEEP

This pose will relieve tired legs and mild backaches as well as provide a gentle stretch for the backs of your legs.

1. Hop into bed and swing your legs up, resting them gently against the headboard (or wall). Squiggle closer until your bottom is as close as is comfortably possible to the headboard. Have your arms by your sides, palms facing up.

2. Lift your hips by bending your knees and pressing your feet onto the headboard. When you lift your hips, slide a pillow under your lower back and the top of your hips to lift them up so that your tailbone curls over the pillow. You want to have a gentle lift of your hips that also allows your lower back to tilt toward the mattress. Your back should feel as if it is arched naturally—this is not a strong arch.

3. Straighten your legs and stay in this position, allowing the blood to rush out of your feet, legs, and hips, giving your heart a rest. This is the perfect time to breathe in and out, focusing your mind on the renewing energy that comes with breath, then focusing on the calm and relaxation that come with quieting the mind and focusing on your breath. Breathe peace in...breathe frustration out.

Stay in this position for 5 minutes while you practice long, slow breaths. This is also a nice pose for practicing gratitude: say a prayer of thanksgiving no matter what kind of day you had. If you can truly feel thankful for even a bad day, you will be on your way to enjoying really good sleep.

MEDITATE ON COOKING

Cooking is a wonderful opportunity for calming your mind and being mindful. There are many small details to attend to while cooking, and you can focus on every one of them. We connect with the earth in a wonderful way as we handle the produce that comes to us from the soil we walk upon. We feel the life around us and give thanks for the food that sustains us so we can continue to flourish each day. We can say a mindfulness prayer as we start our preparations for a home-cooked meal. We can say thanks for the earth that feeds us, the sun that supports us, the seeds that provide for us. We can eat everything that we prepare and waste nothing at all. We can become more economical in our cooking—so waste is a word of the past—and learn to value every morsel that we are fortunate enough to ingest. Our hearts can be filled with gratitude as we make our meals and eat them, focusing our full attention on each and every task.

RELAX INTO RECLINING POSE

Reclining Pose is a great option when you have 5 minutes to spare and you're in your car.

1. Slide your seat back as far as it will go and recline it.
2. Bring your knees toward your chest and place your feet on the dashboard (on either side of the steering wheel) or bring them up toward your chest, wrapping your arms around them. If you have one available, place a rolled towel or sweater behind your neck. If this doesn't work very well in your driver's seat or if the posture leaves you feeling too exposed or vulnerable, move to the passenger side or the back seat.
3. Once you are comfortable, notice your energy and your inner dialogue. If your inner dialogue feels judgmental (of yourself or others), visualize your breath entering the dialogue. Search for words that bring peace to you. They could be: *It is not the end of the world if I do not watch my kid's soccer practice* or *I am not responsible for everyone's happiness*. Think or say these words aloud several times to see if they help shift your inner dialogue. Remember, even a tiny shift will bring you peace.

PART 3

CALM YOUR LIFE

MINDFULLY PREPARE FOR YOUR DAY

You can be mindful about anything, even brushing your teeth! It's as easy as slowing down your morning routine and performing each step with intention and focus, as though every single thing you do is the most important thing you have to do in your life. If you're new to mindfulness, it helps to focus on your breath for a few minutes and use that focus to quiet your mind. Then, gather your senses and bring your full consciousness to what you are doing. Physically slow down, paying attention to sensory input, such as the feel of your clothing as it glides over your skin or the sound of the water running when you brush your teeth. If your mind wanders, always go back to focusing on your breath. This may feel awkward at first, but what you want to avoid is habitually (and unconsciously) rushing through these activities. As you are brushing your teeth, for example, try not to think about your next activity. Instead, bring all your attention to what's happening in that moment: the feel of the brush as you use it to massage your gums and clean your teeth, the way your mouth feels sparkling clean after you rinse. Isn't it great that you have teeth to brush? Smile at yourself in the mirror!

Mindfulness is about staying focused on what's happening right here, right now, avoiding thoughts of the past or the future. In the preceding example, you just breathe and brush...breathe and brush. It's also about savoring experiences and feeling gratitude for your blessings.

BE READY FOR ANYTHING MEDITATION

The first few minutes before everyone else gets out of bed can be perfect "me time," at least enough time for you to de-clutter your mind with this simple, quick meditation. The idea of this meditation is "nonthinking," which is emptying all the thoughts that sprang to attention and started marching around your gray cells the minute you awakened (most of which probably have to do with other people and not yourself). If you take a few minutes to clear your mind, you'll have a much better chance of being able to hear the wisdom of the universe (God, your particular higher power, source of creativity, or divinity). Take a few minutes to simply be still and quiet your mind, and the reassurance and energy you need will come.

Choose a place that is clean and uncluttered. Better yet, go to your sacred space. It's best not to eat anything first, as you want your body to feel comfortable rather than be busily digesting whatever you've grabbed on the run. Plus, meditating first will improve your digestion, and after you have centered yourself, you will also be more likely to choose to mindfully indulge in a healthy breakfast.

1. Begin by removing your slippers or socks so your feet can breathe. Those lovely feet that take you everywhere have thousands of nerve endings. Those nerve endings stimulate energy and health within your entire body, so always give them their

due by welcoming them to the meditation and giving them an opportunity to participate.

2. Sit on the floor, drawing your legs in to create a folded, cross-legged posture. If you have trouble crossing your legs in a seated position, slip a folded blanket or pillow under your hips to help support your back. If that is not comfortable, sit against a wall with your back straight and your legs extended, or sit on a chair.

3. Once you are in this position, slowly straighten your spine, raising the crown of your head toward the ceiling and tucking your chin in slightly.

4. Once your spine is lengthened, relax your shoulders by dropping them down away from your ears and slowly moving your shoulder blades backward and toward each other. Although you want this to be a relaxed posture, it may help to imagine that you are loosely folding your shoulder blades around a grapefruit or a small ball.

5. Close your eyes or just lower your gaze.

6. Relax your hands onto your knees, palms up, or, if you would like, place your hands in your lap, palms up, and then bring your thumb and first finger together to form a *guyan* mudra. This is a sacred Buddhist symbol in which the thumb represents the soul of the universe and the finger represents your own soul. Touching them together represents a union of the two energies, which helps clear your mind, improve alertness, and enhance clarity.

7. Inhale slowly through your nose...exhale slowly through your mouth. Keep breathing until you achieve a natural rhythm in which the slow inhalation and the slow exhalation are approximately the same length.
8. Spend several minutes doing nothing except focusing on your breath. If thoughts arise, do your best to ignore them, returning your attention to your breath. If it helps, when thoughts arise (and they will), silently remind your brain that you are choosing to release all thoughts and clear your mind. Soon you'll be able to achieve this without prompts from your mind to your brain.
9. When you feel centered, calm, and grounded in your being, uncross your legs, bring your knees together, and slowly roll onto your side. Wrap your arms around your legs and pull them toward you, giving yourself a hug, and then release and slowly stand.

As you move into your day, use your breath as a way to bring your attention back to the feeling you experienced during the meditation. You should be ready to handle anything life throws your way.

HAVE A CUP OF TEA

In the midafternoon, take a moment to indulge in a refreshing cup of tea—and do a mindfulness meditation while you're at it.

Teatime is about using all your senses. Use your favorite teacup or even your good china for teatime. Pampering yourself adds to the relaxation and refreshment you'll derive from a mindful meditation.

1. Pour hot water over a teabag into a teapot or directly into your cup. Let it sit for a few minutes.
2. Look at the color of the tea. Is it gold, perhaps? Think about the color gold. What does this bring up? Stay with positive thoughts: flecks of gold in your child's eyes, the gold of a sunset or a summer flower, a gold wedding ring, or any positive associations.
3. Lean over and smell the scent of the tea. Deeply inhale the scent of the tea and bring the cup up to your lips. Before you sip, pause to feel the warmth and breathe it in.
4. Slowly sip the tea, using your taste buds and sense of smell to focus on the tea. What flavors are present? Can you taste flowers or herbs? If it's not too hot, hold a sip of tea in your mouth for a few seconds and truly savor the subtle flavors.

Use all your senses to enjoy your tea, as though it were the first cup of tea you have ever experienced.

HUG IT OUT MEDITATION

This is an excellent meditation to do with your children. For small children, lie together on a bed, wrap your arms around them. Recreate a very soft "ocean breath" by breathing through your nose and making the sound of "Haaaaa." Tell them that mother dogs exhale through their nose with a full breath like this to calm their puppies; when the puppies hear this breath, they know it is time to settle down. Have your children join in as you all breathe like the ocean (or a mamma dog soothing her puppies), and they will calm down in minutes. You can then use this same technique in other stressful situations.

For older kids, wrap your arms around them and pull them in for a firm hug. Envision your two hearts melding. This will be good for both of you.

GET RID OF TEMPTATION

Don't have bad habit triggers in your house. If sugar sets you off on a binge, don't keep sugary snacks around. If you can't resist shopping, leave your credit card at home—bring just enough cash to make your purchase and no more. Don't keep alcohol in the house if that's your weakness. If nighttime TV is your weakness, get that TV out of your bedroom. Take 5 minutes today and look around your home or workspace and look for a temptation you have. Whatever it is that tempts you—a certain kind of food, your emergency pack of cigarettes—get rid of it. Why leave yourself open to continuing to fall into a bad habit when you can just rid yourself of the trigger and breathe a sigh of relief knowing that you no longer have easy access to something that harms your mental or physical health.

MIRROR ME

Here's a fun meditation you can try with a child or a partner.

1. Sit cross-legged on the floor with your child or partner facing you. Have your knees lightly touching.
2. Both of you should bring up your hands and you should hold your hands about a half-inch away from your child's hands.
3. Tell your child you're going to move your hands in circles really slowly and that his task is to mirror your motions. Start off slowly and simply, but expand the circles and add some wackiness to make it fun. Before you know it, you will both be collapsing with laughter.
4. Take turns being the mirror, encouraging all kinds of shapes and swirls to see if you can keep up with each other. Mirror meditation works because mirroring takes concentration and will calm frayed nerves...and it's just a whole lot of fun!

BUILD A PERSONAL SANCTUARY

After a long day at work, you come home to your castle, your haven of peace and comfort and...a pile of dirty laundry, a mound of dirty dishes, a stack of newspapers to be sorted through and recycled, footprints in the kitchen...and oh, no! There are those books you were supposed to return yesterday. Suddenly, it doesn't seem so relaxing to be home.

But coming home doesn't have to be stressful. Coming home at the end of the day or staying home all day long can be a relaxing, peaceful, even positively exhilarating experience if that's what you want it to be. If your home isn't the place you want it to be, it may just require a little stress management.

According to feng shui, the ancient Chinese art of placement, our environment is a metaphor for our lives and the energy that comes and goes in our lives. Problems in your environment mean problems in your life.

Consider this idea for a moment. If your home is a metaphor for your life, how does your life look? Take a good look around you. Is your life cluttered with stuff you don't need? How's the circulation? How long has it been since you've done preventive maintenance on your life?

Whether you work from home or in an office building, your office can also be a metaphor for your life. Is your life scattered with unpaid bills, things to file, scraps of information that take up energy but don't give anything back, malfunctioning equipment, or unstable piles of books, files, binders, and folders?

If your home or office space doesn't exactly reflect how you would like your life to look, then take matters into your own hands. Let your home and office continue to be a metaphor for your life, but shape that metaphor in a way that suits your life. Remove the clutter. Keep your space clean. Build a relaxing, positive atmosphere where you can decompress at the end of each day.

To make your home a less stressful, more tranquil place, one of the easiest things you can do is simplify. Spend 5 minutes in each room of your home and list all the things you do in each room. What are the functions of the room? What would make each room simpler, its functions simpler?

Simplify your cleaning chores by creating a system for getting everything done by doing a little bit each day. Simplify your shopping by buying in bulk and planning your menu a week in advance. You can simplify the way your home works—and consequently reduce your stress whenever you're at home—in many ways.

MAKE MORE SPACE

Some people feel comforted by a room full of stuff, but there is something relaxing and calming about a clean, clutter-free space. Why not put away or give away some of that stuff and free up some space? As you make space on your surfaces, floors, and walls and in your rooms, you'll feel like you are making space in your mind. You'll feel more relaxed and calmer in that clean, organized, uncluttered space. If you donate items, you'll also get the feeling of satisfaction that comes from helping others. Or if you sell clothing or other items on consignment, you can make a little pocket money.

Clutter does more than keep your home, desk, or garage looking messy—clutter keeps your mind messy too. The more stuff you have (especially disorganized, unmatched, lost, or high-maintenance stuff), the more you have to worry about it, find it, maintain it, keep it, deal with it, have it. Spend 5 minutes today making one area of your life a little less messy. Maybe you could donate those books you never even unpacked, maybe you could recycle those old magazines gathering dust in the corner, maybe you could empty out all the old food from your fridge. Even small changes made daily will start to add up and before you know it you'll have more space. Getting rid of the clutter in your home is the most important thing you can do to make your home a stress-free haven of tranquility.

CREATE A SACRED SPACE

While you can meditate anywhere, having a sacred space is ideal. The word *sacred* in this sense simply means a place where you feel comfortable reconnecting with your inner self and spirit. Ideally, it is a place in your home that affords privacy and quiet, a place where you can keep your sacred objects, such as candles or beloved objects that represent something deeply meaningful to you.

- Find a space in your home where you can meditate. Where do you naturally go that feels peaceful? It can be in any room of the house, or it can be a small space within a room. Use your intuition to choose a space that feels warm, inviting, and peaceful. Claim it as your own.
- Have a cushion or soft rug you can comfortably sit on. If you are not comfortable sitting on the floor, a chair is fine. You may also want a yoga mat, as many meditations are yoga poses (combining physical, mental, and spiritual meditation).
- Create an altar where you can place objects that hold meaning for you. This can be as simple as a pretty cloth or scarf draped over a small table with a vase of flowers, a beautiful shell, a piece of your mother's jewelry, or something your children gave you. These items will help you transition from the noise and chaos that usually reign over our busy lives to a place of quiet and

contemplation. You might want to light a candle and listen to some soft music. Some people like to use a watch or timer if their time for meditating is truly limited. (Tip: using your cell phone alarm—set to a pleasant tone and at a super low volume—may not feel as intrusive as other timers.)

EMBRACE THE HIDDEN COMMUNITY

If you usually practice meditation alone, take a few moments to remind yourself that there are thousands of other people around the world learning meditation too. Embracing this community will allow you to share your positive energy and will keep you motivated.

1. Practice deep breathing for 2 minutes with this pattern: inhale for twelve counts, hold for six, exhale for twelve, and hold for six. During this time, picture your inner self opening to the cosmos: expectant, loving, and serene.
2. During the next 3 minutes of this meditation, think of others around the world who are struggling to establish themselves in the practice of meditation just as you are. Send these fellow travelers the same positive energy that you have experienced in your meditation. Wish them success in all their material and spiritual endeavors. Picture their physical bodies healed of any health conditions they may be facing and wish them vibrant health and longevity. See their questions answered and their problems solved. Know that others are wishing the same for you; feel this hidden support for all that you do too.
3. Once you have finished your meditation, consider reaching out to others who are on the path of meditation through a web posting, email, or phone call.

RELEASE TENSION WITH OSTRICH POSE

This pose is called Ostrich because ostriches sleep with their heads buried in the sand. Try this pose with a partner.

1. Stand with your backs toward each other and with your feet apart. If there are more than two of you, stand in a circle with your backs toward the center. ·
2. Inhale and reach your hands up toward the ceiling.
3. Exhale and fold forward, hands touching or reaching toward the floor. Stay folded over while you look at each other. You can even make silly faces. Anytime you can share smiles and laughter, tension will lighten.

PERFORM HALF-MOON POSE

Half-Moon Pose opens the chest, shoulders, and torso while also lengthening the spine.

1. Stand really tall. If there are more than two of you performing this pose, stand in a circle facing toward each other.
2. Reach your arms up as high as you are able.
3. Reach over to one side so that your body looks like a half-moon.
4. Straighten, then reach over to the other side with both arms.
5. Keep bending right, then left, until you feel ready to move on.

STRETCH INTO FROG POSE

This is a fun pose and really good for opening and stretching the hips, groin, and insides of the thighs.

1. Starting on all fours, walk your knees as far apart as you comfortably can without straining. The insides of your feet should be touching the ground and your legs should be bent at 90-degree angles.
2. Inhale and elongate your spine by extending your head and tailbone in opposite directions.
3. Exhale and slowly lower yourself down onto your forearms, making sure your elbows are stacked below your shoulders.
4. Allow your hips to draw back and down. Stay here for 5 breaths.

PRAY SLOWLY

Slowing down can bring you to a place of acceptance—acceptance of who you are and what you have, acceptance of your family, your friends, your financial situation, your community, and the world. Slowing down can become a meaningful, mindful practice. Here's how you can slow down the act of preparing to pray to get into a mindful state.

1. Come to a comfortable cross-legged posture on a rug or a yoga mat. Inhale and exhale slowly until your breath feels very natural.
2. Shake your hands rapidly, then rest your hands on your knees, palms upward. Bring all your awareness to your fingertips. Feel the tip of each and every finger and thumb. As you think of each finger, move it just slightly. You may feel almost a pulse or a throbbing sensation at your fingertips.
3. Very slowly lift your hands off your knees, bringing them toward each other. Feel as though the space between your hands is thick. Move as slowly as you are able, as though your hands were moving themselves. Notice the tiniest detail of the movement.
4. Bring your hands together in front of your heart center and press your thumbs into the center of your sternum. Stay for a few minutes in slowness.
5. When you are ready, pray slowly, with true intention.

DON'T LISTEN TO OTHERS' NEGATIVITY

As you begin your meditation practice, you may find that some people get defensive when they hear about it. They will say things like "Oh, I have a short attention span; I could never focus like that" or "I could never sit still for that long." Of course, these same people can sit and watch a feature-length film with no problem or surf the Internet for hours on end. The real problem is not a short attention span—it's how your attention is directed and to what end.

If you're accustomed to activity and passivity, the idea of receptivity—the basis of meditation—can be uncomfortable. We notice the big, flashy things rather than the small, quiet things. Our senses are burned out by a constant barrage of images and sounds. The mental shell-shock of living in a consumer society means we have a hard time dealing with real space and time.

Don't listen to naysayers who try to put you off your path. Instead stay focused on your goals, try to surround yourself with positive, supportive people, and take daily action toward your goal. Research has shown that action taken daily rather than sporadically leads to sustained change, so remember to meditate for at least 5 minutes a day to find your inner calm and help banish those negative voices.

TAKE REFUGE DURING DIFFICULT TIMES

If you've ever had a migraine headache, you know that your best relief is a dark, quiet room. It doesn't take the pain away, but it makes it easier to wait it out. The refuge helps you separate yourself from the pain, to observe it as though it does not belong to you. The same can be said of meditation: in painful times, your inner self can be that dark room, a portable place of retreat you always have with you. You won't be able to make problems go away by sheer force of will, but you can stop identifying with them. In this way, they become less solid and real, as though you were watching them in a movie.

The next time you are feeling overwhelmed by events in your life, turn off all your devices, turn off all your lights, draw your curtains or blinds, and sit in the quiet of a dark room for 5 minutes. Shut yourself away from the world and just focus on your breath and the stillness of the dark. This won't make your tough situation go away, but it will help you be better equipped to deal with it.

STIMULATE YOUR SECOND CHAKRA

Opening and stimulating your second chakra will help you renew your creative energy. This is great if you are in the middle of a project and have lost your creative energy or if you just want to start a project with a creative intent.

1. Stand with your feet slightly more than hip-width apart, keeping your knees slightly bent.
2. Bring your hands to your knees.
3. Exhale as you round your spine, bringing your chin to your chest. Tilt the bottom of your pelvis forward.
4. Inhale as you reverse this position: arch your back, look up, and stick your chest out.
5. Continue tilting and arching for about 3 minutes.

When you feel ready, proceed to working on your creative project, feeling as if you have literally primed your creative pump (because you have!).

TAKE A MOMENT WITH YOUR KIDS

When you serve your children breakfast, take a moment to kneel beside each: tousle his hair, kiss her cheek, or simply say a heartfelt "Good morning, darling." Savor the moment. Make eye contact, breathe in and out slowly, and smile. Pausing for even a single beat will help both you and your child connect. It may even become the favorite part of the day for both of you. Remember, mindfulness is not about judgment or pressure, and it's not just another thing you have to do. These are moments to savor simply being alive and, in this case, having a relationship with your children.

MAKE PLANS FOR LATER

Anticipation is almost as much fun as an actual experience. Did you know that if you visualize a future event (or past event) in detail, as if it's happening in real time, your brain will believe the event is actually happening? That means you get to enjoy the experience twice!

If you're having a rough day, taking 5 minutes to visualize a planned event you'll enjoy—having dinner with your family, seeing a movie with friends, going on a long-awaited vacation—can really brighten your day.

Build the visualization by coming to a quiet place, then think about the details: Whom will you be with? Where will you be? What will you be doing? Imagine the tastes and smells and textures, the sounds and sights. If you're visualizing dinner with your family, imagine your children's faces as they tell you about their day or help you fix the meal. Feel the good feelings—as if they were already happening—and before you transition back into your daily schedule, end your visualization by stating an intention to mindfully enjoy the upcoming experience.

FIND PEACE

If you always try to make sense of things, you sometimes make them worse. When you stop trying to solve everything, however, you can find peace. Peace is not a matter of rainbows, unicorns, or cute puppies, nor is peace some sort of sentimental or naive way of looking at the world. Rather, peace is a matter of divesting yourself of harmful thoughts and feelings, a subtracting process of peeling away layers of mental buildups. While meditation is the best way to find peace sometimes in your busy life you may not have the time or gumption to sit calmly and meditate. So how can you find peace in 5 minutes? The key is to practice a kind of meditation on the go. Certain activities that you have to do in your daily life can become a kind of meditation that can help you empty your mind and strip away those unneeded thoughts. For 5 minutes today try to do something slightly repetitive that doesn't require a lot of thinking. Maybe a chore like washing the dishes, chopping vegetables, sweeping the floor, or a practiced hobby like knitting. Do this activity in a quiet place with no distractions if possible and simply focus on your senses as you do it. This mental slowdown may be just the thing you need to get rid of the thoughts that are weighing you down and help you find some peace.

SURRENDER

A kind of surrender takes place in meditation. You realize your own mortality and vulnerability, your own powerlessness. In difficult times, you can convert sorrow into sweet sorrow, the kind that reminds you that you are still alive. It may be scant consolation, but it may also keep you from deeper distress or despair. All too often we magnify our bad situations by dwelling on them. Meditation gives us ease because it helps us let go of these situations.

During the rough spots, sometimes the best thing you can do is take a step back and try to calm your frayed nerves. Meditation can be the quiet refuge that makes a seemingly untenable situation bearable. It can change the emotional filter through which you view the world, making your burdens seem lighter. When you stub your toe first thing in the morning and then spill your coffee, everything seems irritating for the rest of the morning: traffic lights seem to conspire against you, file folders rebel against your clumsy fingers, and the sound of a ringing phone makes you want to scream.

This frustrated, persecuted feeling has no roots in reality—instead, it is formed by a mental process in which the world becomes negatively shaded. By contrast, if you can take a few minutes in your day to deliberately cultivate peace and compassion, you'll notice traffic on the way to work seems to flow better, that annoying colleague just seems amusing rather than psychotic, and the leftovers you brought for lunch are the best thing you have ever eaten. This is not the wild optimism of intention manifestation or wish fulfillment or magical thinking; it is just the simple observation that our mental state changes the way we see the world. Gently adjusting your mental state can give you the strength you need to keep going, which might be just enough to help you find a solution.

CALM DOWN IN THE CAR

We spend a lot of time in our cars. Often, there are things going on in your car that can distract you from proper driving: maybe your kids are fighting, maybe you get an annoying phone call, maybe other drivers are causing you distress. Whatever the reason, you need to calm down so you can safely operate your vehicle. If you can, pull over to the side of the road, park your car, and take a few moments to simply breathe.

It turns out that your mother was right: counting to ten is actually a very effective mini–meditation/breathing exercise to quell emotions and regain your center. Inhale as you count to ten...exhale as you count backward from ten to one:

- Inhale: one, two, three, four, five, six, seven, eight, nine, ten.
- Exhale: ten, nine, eight, seven, six, five, four, three, two, one.

Repeat a few times. If you like, you can chant the sound of "Om": inhale deeply and open your mouth wide; then, as you exhale, form the short-vowel sound "Aaaaaa," then the long-vowel sound "Oooooo" as you begin closing your mouth, then "Mmmmmm" as you finish closing your mouth. The sound should vibrate in your mouth.

Maybe you can make your kids laugh by pointing out that they make similar sounds when they wail "Oh, Mom!" All they have to do to say "Om" is really drag it out, chanting "Oooohhhhhhmmmmmoooommmm."

IGNORE THE NOISE

What if you are driving and you can't pull over to calm down? Blotting out the noise is a viable option. While driving, you have to keep your focus on the road ahead, so focus even harder. Find a way to drown out the kids' squabbling with a positive mantra. A mantra is a sound or word you say over and over to create something, usually a change or a healing. It can be anything you would like it to be. Think of a mantra as a prayer. You don't have to say it aloud, although you can go that route if you like. Here are a few mantras you could try:

- *May I have peace within my heart, peace with all my relationships, and peace with all beings.*
- *Nothing will distract me from driving safely.*
- *Love is all I need to get through my day.*
- *I hear joyful noises and feel love all around me.*

Whatever you do, make them positive mantras, as they have a way of becoming part of your reality and manifesting what you say you want. If you practice a religion, certain prayers or lines of prayers may resonate with you. Otherwise, spend some time creating powerful, positive mantras that you can use in trying situations—and when you're meditating.

SLIP INTO YOUR FAVORITE PAJAMAS

Take a few minutes, sneak away from family members if you have to, and slip into your favorite pajamas, whether they're made of wispy cotton or snuggly flannel. As you change, take a few minutes to smooth a refreshing, scented (or unscented) oil or lotion over your arms, legs, neck, and back. Pause to take a breath and inhabit your body fully. Notice any tension, then gently massage painful areas. End by massaging your feet and then your hands with lotion or oil. Using your thumb to massage your hands is very relaxing. If you have a partner, you can give each other a mini-massage.

TALK TO A FRIEND

Find a friend whom you can trust, with whom you can speak candidly and truthfully, someone who is caring and has a genuine concern for your needs and feelings, someone who has a sense of humor. How great to be able to laugh at yourself and not take yourself too seriously!

A true friend will encourage, accept, and support you, no matter what is happening in your life. We all have a need for true friendship, to receive it and to give it as well. Once you have a trusted friend, you can prearrange a convenient time for a phone conversation (or call her when emotional emergencies occur). Always make sure you are comfortable—maybe you have your feet up and a cup of tea within reach—before calling your friend. Don't use the phone call as an opportunity to vent! Instead, think of it as a meditation, a talking meditation that will help you relieve stress and feel grounded. Choose to mindfully talk with your friend, asking for her support during a stressful time, mindfully connecting with someone who understands and cares about you.

LOOK FOR SMALL HOLES IN YOUR SCHEDULE

Sure, you're busy. We all are. But the average day is not a solid wall of activity—it's more like Swiss cheese. The key to finding a little bit of personal time is to look for the small pockets of air. Remember, we're talking about only a few minutes at a time. Most people don't have the luxury of long blocks of time, but nearly everyone can find a 5-minute block.

When you identify a space of personal time in your day, schedule it on your calendar. Commit to it in writing. Then, when you come to the appointed time, drop everything and get settled for meditation. Be aware that something will happen that might tempt you to deviate from the plan: you might get a phone call from a client, a deadline might be changed, your email might ping repeatedly. Discriminate between the true emergencies that need your attention and the routine miasma of noise that you can tune out.

Maybe you have trouble distinguishing between emergencies and noise. Ask yourself, "Can this wait for a few minutes? Will my reputation be affected if I don't attend to this right this minute?" Tell yourself you can get right back to whatever issue arises as soon as the meditation is over. You may even have a better handle on the issue after meditating than you would have before.

If you're still having trouble letting go, meditate anyway. It is better to meditate while distracted than not meditate at all. If you miss a session because you just can't drop what you are doing, no worries—just get yourself back on track at the next appointed time.

Don't feel the need to atone for a missed session by adding that time to a future session. Guilt-tripping is not productive! This is about your own unfolding development, not some imaginary yardstick of perfection. If you miss a session, it just means that's where you were at that moment in your journey. Don't cry over lost time or a difficult session. If you have discovered meditation as part of the purpose for your life and not just an adjunct to it, you are not in danger of losing it entirely—you will return to it at a later time, when your life atmosphere is more conducive to meditating.

STAYING BALANCED WITH MOODY TEENAGERS

Some of the most effective strategies for dealing with sulky or rebellious teenagers include ignoring their behavior, killing them with kindness, or making them laugh. The point is to not buy into their negative moods or reinforce their bad manners. The main thing is to stay calm and mindful.

If you need a breather to calm down, try this:

1. Remove yourself from the situation and slow down your breathing until you feel calmer.
2. Go to your sacred space and meditate for 5 minutes. Often all you need to do is release pent-up feelings, let go of any resentment over mishaps that occurred, and re-center yourself so that you can enjoy your family's company.
3. As you release your feelings of frustration, take a step back and remind yourself that although the present may feel stressful, in the future, you'll look back on these times with fondness.
4. Reflect on your own teenage years, remembering how close to the surface your emotions felt in those years and how difficult it was for you to keep a steady perspective.
5. Repeat an affirmation or intention about engaging mindfully with your teenager. For example, you could say, "My teen needs me to model calmness so that she can learn to regulate her own emotions" or "I will go forward from a place of stillness to engage thoughtfully with my child."

MAXIMIZE YOUR FREE MOMENTS

The ancient Greeks distinguished between *chronos* and *kairos*—time as it is measured in days and time as it is measured in experience. *Chronos* flows in a linear, regular fashion, while *kairos* has connotations of an appropriate or fortuitous hour. When you manage *chronos* effectively, *kairos* will toss a few freebies your way: the big meeting will be canceled, the server will go down, or the boss will catch the flu. Without taking advantage of these gifts of time in a deceptive manner, you can use them to meditate and boost your productivity.

Consciously take control of your time and see this free hour as the gift that it is. Maybe this extra time could be used to push yourself a little further than you would ordinarily go in your practice, or maybe you could read an article or book that would improve your technique. Perhaps you could go outside for a walk or look into a weekend retreat.

One reason people don't feel more rested is because they fill their breaks with more information and more noise. Your brain may not process a blog post all that much differently from a work report. Reading the blog might be a marginally better option if you derive happiness from it, but you are still engaging visual processing, language centers, and other parts of your brain. If you are trying to write the report and work on the blog post at the same time, you are definitely adding stress to your life. In order for the brain to truly rest, you have to ratchet down the level of activity. Meditation provides a real rest for the brain because meditation brings the brain down to a baseline state while simultaneously calming respiration and circulation.

Putting a 5-minute meditation break into your routine is like putting a period at the end of a sentence: it lets you pause and wind down from what came before in order to prepare for what is coming next. Running on full throttle at all times creates confusion and stress.

STOP EVERYTHING

Every day brings with it a big to-do list. However, on those days when "too much to do" reaches the level of "insanely overbooked, over-stressed, and freaking out," it's time to stop everything. That's right: don't do anything. Stop all thoughts. Stop the mind chatter. What you need to maintain your sanity is to take a breather. This mindfulness meditation will help you stop and let go so that you're ready to tackle the insanity.

1. Lie down on a rug or yoga mat. With your legs extended, take a few falling-out breaths: inhale through your nose and exhale while saying "Haaaa."
2. Bring your knees toward your chest and hug your knees for another few breaths.
3. Let your arms go out to the sides and be sure that your feet are touching the mat with your knees bent. Inhale...exhale.
4. As you exhale, bring your knees over to the right and look to the left. Stay in this position for a few breaths. Inhale...exhale.
5. As you exhale, bring your knees to the left and look to the right.
6. Think of your body as a giant kitchen sponge and visual-ize yourself wringing out all your chattering thoughts. Twist from side to side slowly, and as you do, exhale and wring out everything.

If your mind resists and you are not able to stop the mind chatter, create the intention to replace the chattering with breath. Once you are "wrung out," you are ready to absorb quiet and peace. Be patient with this intention, remaining in the meditation until you feel refreshed.

BATTLE STRESS WITH YOGA

This pose is perfect—physically and psychologically—for dealing with stresses. It helps develop balance, steadiness, and poise.

1. Stand with your feet hip-width apart. Feel the four corners of each foot pressing evenly into the floor. (Weather permitting, this is a great pose to do outside with bare feet.) Lengthen your spine and lift the crown of your head toward the ceiling (or the sky if you're practicing outside). Gently engage your leg muscles, especially lifting your quad muscles. Lift your pelvic floor by pulling up the muscles (as though you were trying not to pee) and engage your abdomen by pulling your stomach muscles inward.

2. Bring the sole of your right foot to the inner thigh of your left supporting leg and open your right knee out to the side. (Feel free to hold onto a chair or counter to help with balance.)

3. Bring your hands together in a prayer position. Look at something that is not moving to help with balance, then focus on your breath until you feel steady. When you do, bring your hands up as though you are a tree extending your branches.

If you are not able to balance today, use this as an opportunity to reflect on what may be out of balance in your life. As you do balancing postures, you may notice that some days you can balance for quite a while and other days not so much. Being mindful is noticing (without judging) the differences from day to day.

DON'T RUSH OUT THE DOOR

Going out to dinner without the kids? Before you leave, spend 5 minutes sitting quietly with your children (including your teenagers, who will appreciate it even if they roll their eyes). It's not about asking permission; it's about connecting with them to let them know that you are going out to enjoy your companion's company, not to get away from them. Ask them what thay have planned for the evening, and suggest something that might be fun for them to do with the babysitter, such as watching their favorite movie, making popcorn, or working on crafts. Give your children a goodnight kiss and tell them you love them. All too often we rush out the door, when stopping for just a brief second to connect would lead to the kind of warm, loving feelings that make a world of difference.

PRE-PARTY CALM

You are about to have a party and you feel your nerves starting to act up. Here is a great way to quickly relax before your guests arrive. Light a candle and put it on the dinner table, then then take 5 minutes to do a simple meditation.

1. Make sure the candle is directly in front of you, at eye level if possible.
2. Close your eyes and sit at the table with your spine lengthened. It helps to sit at the very edge of the chair with your feet planted firmly on the floor—that way, you won't be tempted to lean back on the chair.
3. Open your eyes and gaze at the candle flame for about 1 minute. Bring all your concentration to just the candle flame and nothing else. All awareness is in the flame.
4. Notice how the flame jumps around with just a hint of a breeze. Notice the colors of the flame...how it is blue at the base and yellow, red, and white at the top. See how the colors change. If your mind begins to chatter or you get distracted, bring your awareness back to the flame. See it with a child's eye, as though for the first time.
5. Now close your eyes, but in your mind's eye, keep looking at the flame. If you forget exactly how it looks, open your eyes for a second and then close them again. Stay with this candle meditation for about 5 minutes.

6. When the 5 minutes are almost over, think about who is coming for dinner. Consider a toast for your guests—a toast of gratitude for friendship, for the meal you are serving, and for good health.

When your guests show up, stop everything you are doing and greet them at the door. Give each of your guests a really big hug, bringing your hands onto the back of their heart centers. Even if you are not a hugger, you will be offering an amazing gift to your guests.

SEEK OUT MEDITATION COMMUNITIES

Some of the great meditation schools—spiritual, contemplative, and devotional—offer meditation training. Some offer short retreats, a few days away from the outside world. These sessions are useful for the busy person. Other schools offer extended training periods, perhaps for a month or more, to develop specific meditation techniques. Students who attend these courses may receive certification or initiation into the discipline. Although you may not intend to teach meditation techniques in the near future, participating in training events is a great way to acquire a comprehensive view of meditation. As you put your new information into practice, you will appreciate the depth of experience that you can acquire during longer sessions.

Retreats are another opportunity to experience meditation under the guidance of one or more leaders. Attending just one retreat can advance your practice more than several months of solo practice during everyday life. Organized retreats surround you with all the components of meditation even if you have been unable to establish them in your regular life: quiet time, peaceful surroundings, well-selected music and readings, and people of like minds all create an ideal meditation experience.

Ashrams and monasteries often open their facilities to part-time residents. Preparing the community's food, caring for the living quarters, and completing tasks in the library or school are activities that are expected of the student in addition to worshipping, studying, and meditating. The retreat attendee becomes part of the discipline of the community and leaves a different person than the one who entered. If you are looking for a place to take a retreat, spend about 5 minutes searching for "monastery," "ashram," or "retreat" along with the name of the desired state or region. You should be able to find a facility nearby. If this doesn't work, consider going on a solitary retreat in a park or national forest.

HIDE THOSE CREDIT CARDS

Some people get a fantastic high from shopping—for some, shopping can become a bad habit and even an addiction. If you head to the store when you are feeling frustrated, depressed, anxious, or worried about something (and if the feeling you get from buying a bunch of stuff really makes you feel better), you can be assured you are shopping for the wrong reason.

Fortunately, a shopping habit can be redirected, just like an overeating habit can be redirected. If you think you shop for the wrong reasons, spend 5 minutes thinking of something else fun to do whenever you feel the shopping impulse. How about something that doesn't cost any money, like going for a walk or taking a soothing bath? It may not feel as satisfying at first, but once you get out of the shopping habit, you'll wonder how you could possibly have spent so much money on so much junk.

QUIT PROCRASTINATING

Procrastinators sometimes despair that procrastination is an ingrained part of their personality and impossible to change. Not true! Procrastination, too, is a habit, and it can be reshaped just like anything else. It will certainly take some doing. Remember that you don't have to stop procrastinating all at once. Choose areas to tackle first, like getting to work on time. How can you reorganize your morning and inspire yourself to get up in the first place? Maybe paying bills on time will be your first focus, or retraining yourself to spend 5 minutes picking up clutter or washing dishes before bedtime. You can do it!

HARNESS IMAGERY POWER

Feeling stressed? Feeling anxious? Go on vacation. No, don't leave your desk and head to the airport. You remember your imagination, don't you? Your imagination is still in your head, even if it's grown a little rusty from disuse. Stay at your desk, but close your eyes, relax, and breathe. For 5 minutes, use your imagination to visualize the place you would most like to be. Why not imagine wandering down a secluded beach at sunset with balmy tropical winds rippling the turquoise sea? Maybe you would prefer cuddling in front of a fire with a special someone in a cozy cabin in the woods? Or maybe images of the Far East, a rain forest, or hiking a glacier in Alaska invoke a sense of peace in you?

AFTER-SCHOOL RECONNECT

An important part of rebalancing after school or work is to truly connect with your kids. Once you are all safely home, convene everyone
in the kitchen for a 5-minute chat before they dash off to do whatever
it is they have to do. Ask your children how their day was, look into
their eyes, listen to their responses, and spark a conversation they'll
enjoy. Softly touching their arms or giving them a warm embrace will
intensify the connection. Note: you don't need food to connect, but if
you choose to offer a healthy snack during these moments, eventually
they'll connect healthy food with happy memories.

PRACTICE THE ABCS OF GRATITUDE

The times when your family is sitting down together for dinner can be the best to learn about and teach gratitude. Studies have shown that those who have the most gratitude are the happiest.

As you are having dinner play this 5-minute gratitude game: start with the letter *A* and think of something you are grateful for that starts with that letter. For example, "I am grateful for apples." Taking turns around the table, go on to the letter *B* and then *C*. Try to make this game silly as well—laughing together can be a beautiful memory. Even if you don't make it all the way through the alphabet in 5 minutes you'll still have made a positive difference and maybe even put a smile on your children's faces.

STAY INSPIRED

When life is stressful, it always seems easier and more manageable if your circumstances can lift you to heights of positive feeling. Staying inspired is key to maintaining the necessary energy, enthusiasm, and motivation for keeping your life on track, your stress in check, and your goals in sight.

For you, staying inspired might mean making a daily commitment to spend a few moments pursuing a beloved hobby, starting your own business, learning something new, taking up an art form, writing a novel, volunteering, or staying in touch with inspiring friends. Whatever keeps you excited about the day, glowing with anticipation, and happy to be alive should be a priority.

TRY A TENSION-RELEASING MEDITATION

To release the tensions of daily life try this meditation:

1. Bring yourself to a comfortable seated posture on the floor with a folded blanket or towel to sit on.
2. Breathe in for the count of five...exhale for the count of seven.
3. Breathe in for the count of five...exhale for the count of seven.
4. Stay with this breath until you are feeling calm (or at least calmer than you were before).
5. Have the intention of letting some things go.
6. Your breath is creating space. You are not able to bring new things into your life until you let some things go.
7. With your eyes closed, notice how you are feeling in your physical body. Notice if you feel tension in your shoulders. Do you hold the weight of the world on your shoulders? With your eyes closed, think about who or what is on your shoulders and causing you to feel weighed down. You may have your entire family lined up on your shoulders. Picture all of them lined up. What else or who else is there? Friends, aging parents, work responsibilities? Take time to really notice all the people and "stuff" you are carrying.
8. Inhale into your belly.
9. Exhale slowly; then, as you lean to your right, reach your right arm straight out and tilt over until your fingertips touch the floor.

10. Watch as everything and everyone slides off your shoulders, joyfully "listening" as they scream "Wheeeee!" while soaring down the slide that is your arm. Let them slide off, trusting that they will be fine, that they don't need to rest on your shoulders.
11. Inhale into your belly.
12. Exhale slowly, then repeat the same motion with your left arm, letting everything and everyone on that side slide off. You may have to shake your arm, as some people will (consciously or unconsciously) hold on really tight, even if everyone (especially you) knows it's good to let them go.

Now that you have let quite a few things go, you can fill up with calm, peace, joy, or whatever you need.

MAKE CHANGES INSTEAD OF EXCUSES

If you're always 5 minutes late in the morning, you're probably experiencing significant stress due to rushing to work each day. You might be inclined to blame the traffic on your commute or to complain that your coffeemaker was on the fritz again, causing you to leave the house later than you should have. These are just excuses. Chances are there is always traffic to deal with, and your coffee pot probably didn't just go on the fritz yesterday. The point is, you're obviously not allowing enough time in the morning to get ready to leave for work. If you woke up just 5 minutes earlier, you'd probably leave the house 5 minutes earlier, and that would help you arrive at the office on time without having to rush and feel stressed. Try it tomorrow and see what good emerges from your day.

APPRECIATE OTHERS

This is a gratitude exercise to help you realize and acknowledge the blessings in your life. When you have your family members all seated together, perhaps for a meal, go around the table and tell each person what you appreciate about him or her. Start with one family member and talk about all the wonderful qualities that person has. Encourage the rest of the family to join you. This can also teach children to be charitable about family members, especially if there is some sibling rivalry. Everyone gets a turn. Don't worry if someone just says one or two words. It takes time to teach how to have gratitude for others in the family. Each person will feel so great being talked about in such a positive and loving way. They will eventually want others to feel the same way and will begin to share their feelings of gratitude for the rest of the family. You could extend this to your pets, telling them how you feel grateful for their unconditional love. Give them an extra rubdown and a treat as you share your gratitude with them.

CALM THE MONEY MADNESS

Every time you are about to spend money, stop for a moment, take a deep breath, and ask yourself, "Do I really want this, or do I just think I want this in this moment?"

Before you spend money, stop for a moment, take a deep breath, and ask yourself, "Is this item worth the time out of my life I took to earn the money I'll pay for it?"

If you decide you really do want something and that it really is worth the money (dinner at a restaurant when you can't face cooking, that one special collector's item you've been seeking for years, that pair of shoes that feels perfect), buying it will probably be less stressful than letting it go.

MANAGE YOUR TIME

Although technically we all have the same amount of time each day (24 hours), time is mysteriously malleable. Have you ever noticed how an hour can fly by like it's 5 minutes or crawl by like it's 3 hours? They say "time flies when you're having fun," but time also flies when you are scattered and disorganized. If you have 3 hours to get something done and you don't manage your time efficiently, those 3 hours will fly by in a rush of half-finished jobs as you flit from task to task with dispersed energy. If, instead, your time is organized and you are able to devote your full concentration to one task at a time, time seems to expand in both quantity and quality.

Start Small

If you start with too many goals, too long of a to-do list, or too high of expectations for yourself, you are setting yourself up for failure. Begin with one single time management step, such as laying out tomorrow's clothes the night before (to save time the next morning) or vowing that the counters will be free of dirty dishes every single night (to ease the breakfast rush). As you master each step, you can add more.

Identify Your Time Management Priorities

Make a list ranking the things on which you most want to spend your time. Would you like to add family time first, then household organization time, then some personal time? Would you like to make time for your favorite hobby, time for yourself, or time for romance? Would you just like more time to sleep?

Look at the top five items on your time management priorities list. Focus on those. Be very wary of taking on anything that occupies your time if that task isn't focused on one of your top five priorities.

SAY NO

Learn to say no to requests for your time unless that time would be spent on something very important to you. You don't have to be on the committee. You don't have to go to that meeting. Just say no and watch the stress that was waiting to descend upon your life float away in another direction.

If you've already taken on too much, learn to start purging. Don't let anything waste your time. Time spent relaxing by yourself isn't wasted if it refreshes and rejuvenates you. Time spent pacing and worrying, however, is wasted time. Time spent enduring a committee meeting you didn't really enjoy is wasted time. In contrast, time spent actively engaged in a committee whose cause inspires you is indeed time well spent.

Take a few minutes today to practice saying no to a demand. Here are some tips:

- If you feel like you can't outright say no to a demand here are some ways to say no diplomatically: "I'm sorry, I can't do that right now," or "It doesn't fit into my schedule."
- If it's a matter of not wanting to be pushed into a commitment right away, try saying, "Let me think about this and get back to you." If you do choose this path make sure you are clear and matter-of-fact and not too promising.
- Say yes to something else, for example, "I can't do that, but I can do..." and mention a lesser commitment that you can make.

VISUALIZE HAPPY MEMORIES

Whenever you begin cooking, spend a few minutes remembering and reconnecting with happy memories you made in the kitchen. Doing so will help calm and center you and help you feel positive about what you're doing.

Think about a time that made you feel particularly good. It could be watching your grandmother make Thanksgiving dinner and helping stir the gravy, helping your mother or father husk corn for corn on the cob, or the time you had a friend over and ended up laughing over the carton of eggs you dropped on the floor.

Hold that memory in your mind. Remember the feelings and sensations. What did it look like and smell like? Who was there with you? Take a moment to really enjoy the memory, then release it with a smile on your face.

MAKE DINNERTIME FUN

If you feel happy and send out happy vibes, your children may be lured into the kitchen to hang out as you cook. If they do join you, give them age-appropriate tasks to do so that they learn how to cooperate and make contributions to family events. (Yes, dinner is an event, even when it's rushed.) Years later, when your children are off living their own lives, you'll look back fondly on these memories. Play your part in making them the kind of memories you'll want them to cherish too.

A few ideas for making dinnertime fun:

- Make a game out of setting the table or use rhymes to help them learn how to set the table.
- Share memories you have of being with your own parents, particularly funny memories.
- Sing songs together.
- Make cookies together and let them lick the spoons!

DO IT LATER

Do you really need to do every single cleaning chore every day? Do you really need to check your email every 10 minutes? Do you really need to change the sheets, vacuum the car, or mow the lawn today? If doing it later is a matter of procrastination, you'll spend your saved time worrying instead of relaxing. But sometimes, when your time is at a premium, you can relieve your stress and make your life easier by postponing less crucial chores. Even though many chores do need to be accomplished, they don't always need to be accomplished right now.

MEDITATE AT WORK

If you have an office with a door that shuts, you have a great scenario for meditating at work. Close the door for 5 minutes and don't feel guilty about it. (Cut your lunch hour short to make up the time if necessary.) If you work in a cubicle, you may not be able to sit on the floor, chant out loud, or light a candle, but you may be able to use headphones to listen to calming music without disturbing your coworkers. If you can't turn off your computer monitor and must sit in front of it, go to an inspiring website (or at least find one that won't be very distracting). If you work on your feet, standing is no particular impediment to the practice of meditation. You can do the exact same exercises while standing, with the added benefit that it will be harder to fall asleep.

If your work environment really is not conducive to meditation at all, you can simply do brief exercises for a few minutes during the day (maybe during a natural break like a lunch hour) and look for longer pauses to meditate when you're not at work.

MEDITATE AT HOME

Meditating at home often presents just as many challenges as meditating at work—you may feel like you're cheating your family if you take a few minutes for yourself, for one thing. But practicing meditation will actually make you more attentive to your family, as well as more patient and loving. You will seem more *there* when you meditate regularly because being more aware and calm means your mind will not be constantly going off in another direction.

The challenge is finding the right practice at the right time. During a very busy period, you may not be able to do seated meditation—you may only be able to breathe deeply while getting dinner on the table or paying bills at your laptop. Usually, though, you can find a few minutes at some point before bed. This might be after you've cleared the dinner dishes or put the kids to bed. You may have to cut back on your TV or social media time, but odds are you can find some time to work on your meditation.

Gradually, your family will come to understand why you are doing what you are doing, and they, too, will see the benefits as you become calmer and more patient.

FIND OTHER PLACES TO MEDITATE

If neither work nor home seems like a suitable location for your meditation practice, think about the other places where you spend time on a daily basis. If you take a train or bus to work, use that time to meditate. If you drive a car to work, practice being mindful while at the wheel. It may save your sanity and even your life!

You could also try meditating while you're running errands. Take a minute or two to collect yourself in the parking lot before going into the store and buying groceries. Or duck into a quiet church or library on your way to drop off the dry cleaning or pick up the dog from the groomer. Use suitable places that already lie along your route. The loss of time will be more than made up for with a greater presence of mind.

CHOP SOME VEGETABLES

Chopping vegetables can be really relaxing and can itself be a mindful meditation. Use it when you're preparing a lot of vegetables for a stir-fry or similar meal.

1. Stand with all the vegetables laid out on the counter in front of you. Line up the vegetables to chop. Make sure you do this slowly and while using all your senses.
   - Look at the colors of the vegetables: the bright orange of the carrots, the green of the broccoli, the white of the onion.
   - Feel the texture of the vegetables: the softness of the silky threads of corn on the cob, the rough skin of carrots, the bumpy eyes of a potato. When was the last time you really appreciated a vegetable?
   - As you chop an onion, enjoy the smell and how it stings your eyes after a while. Notice the great variety of herbs and sample their different smells.
   - Taste a raw vegetable now and then as you are chopping and really appreciate the texture and taste. Sprinkle a little sea salt onto the vegetables as you chop and enjoy the salty raw vegetable.
   - Listen to the sound of the chopping and how it sounds different with each vegetable. While you are cooking, listen to the sounds of simmering and sautéing. Smell the food as it cooks—for example, savor the scent of garlic.

2. Take a moment to really appreciate and give gratitude to everyone who worked to make that food available to you. Offer gratitude to the farmers and workers (who often receive very low wages) who harvest the food, to those who work in factories to produce and prepare packaged food, to the store clerks who sell the food, and so on. The more you offer appreciation and gratitude, the more you will learn to appreciate your many blessings as well as the unknown people who contribute to your blessings.

BUILD YOUR INNER POWER

If you feel the need to build up your stores of confidence and courage, try the yoga Warrior Pose.

1. Stand with your feet about 4 feet apart, turning your right foot to face the right and keeping your left foot facing straight ahead.
2. Hold your arms out straight with one hand pointing right and one pointing left, then turn your torso so that you are looking straight over your right arm. Your right arm, right foot, and face should all be pointing to the right.
3. Bend your right knee and balance your weight between your feet. Hold your arms out strongly and feel the power of the warrior!
4. Repeat to the left.

BE A MENTOR

One of the best ways to feel less stressed is to help somebody else relieve his or her stress. Helping and nurturing other people helps you feel better about yourself. It also helps you regain a sense of purpose and direction, which makes mentoring a great activity for people who have retired from a job that used to provide purpose and direction. Most communities have many opportunities for volunteering in a variety of areas. Spend a few minutes on the Internet looking for a cause that interests you and start helping yourself by helping others.

BE OPEN TO CHANGE

If you are change-resistant, this is a good practice for you. For some people, no change is ever a good change, but change is inevitable in life and is almost always stressful (even if it's the kind of stress that feels good). Becoming more open to change takes an attitude shift. Start by spotting changes and then finding one good thing about every change you experience. Someone parked in your spot? You can get a few extra minutes of exercise by walking from a spot farther away. It's good for your body! Your favorite restaurant is out of your favorite food? What a great opportunity to try something different. Your favorite TV show is preempted? Another opportunity! Spend some time reading a book, taking a walk, or practicing a new stress management technique.

Major changes are even easier. No matter how disturbing it is to you initially, a change can have a positive side, even if you can't find that silver lining right away. But finding the positive side isn't even the most important thing about being open to change—the most important thing is a willingness to accept that, yes, things change, and, yes, you can go with the flow.

DO A DAILY DE-CLUTTER

Whether your house contains mountains of clutter or one messy surface in a back room out of view, clutter attracts stress. Just looking at clutter suggests clutter to the mind. While de-cluttering your entire garage, basement, or bedroom closet may be a monumental task to accomplish all at once, any big de-cluttering job can be accomplished in small steps.

Every day, spend 5 minutes—no more, unless you schedule ahead to spend a larger block of time—de-cluttering something. Maybe it will be that dump-it table by the front door, or the pile of laundry on top of the dryer, or one corner of your desk. Whatever it is, clear something out each day and feel your mind let out a sigh of relief.

PLAY WITH A PET

Consider getting a pet. Pets are proven to reduce stress and can provide you with a lasting and satisfying relationship. Small dogs and cats are easy to handle and give back tenfold what you give them. Birds can also be rewarding companions, and you can teach them to talk!

Spend some quality time with your pet. Pets relieve stress. And because they seem to love you unconditionally, they can make you feel pretty good about yourself too. Every day take a few minutes and cuddle with your pets. Talk to them about the anxiety or stress you've been going through—you'll feel a lot better.

LAUGH

You've heard the old saying that "Laughter is the best medicine," right? It's more than just a cliché—there is actual science behind it. Laughter and smiling releases endorphins, which help fight stress and make you feel more relaxed. Whether you are watching a TV show or reading a book, laughter is a great form of stress relief and can physically help your body as well. Laughter increases you intake of oxygen-rich air, which can stimulate your heart, lungs, and muscles. Laughter also stimulates circulation and muscle relaxation, both of which can help reduce the physical symptoms of stress. So each day, take a few minutes and find a way to laugh about your own situations...and watch your stress begin to fade.

RELAX ON CUE

You can make yourself relax quickly by associating relaxation with a cue.

1. Get comfortable, breathe deeply, and repeat a word or sound that has positive associations for you ("love," "yellow," "ahhh") out loud for 1 minute as you concentrate on relaxing.
2. Do this several times every day for a week with the same word, then try saying that word whenever you feel stress mounting. You'll feel your body relax automatically!

LOOK AT THE PERSON IN THE MIRROR

Most people focus on external features, but gazing at your "beyond" reflection in a mirror can be a form of meditation. For a few minutes today, gaze into your own eyes, deeper and deeper until you no longer recognize your features but you can see the self behind the eyes. This is both an exercise for relieving stress through focusing and a technique for pursuing self-knowledge.

TAKE A REFLECTION WALK

This strategy is for people who (a) don't get enough exercise on most days and (b) tend to worry too much or mentally obsess about negative things in their lives. You know who you are! A reflection walk is a way to proactively take control of your physical and mental state. If you worry all day, sit at a desk all day, or feel rotten all day, then you need a daily reflection walk, and you need it badly. You can pretend to be an active optimist for a few minutes. And even though you may have to pretend at first, eventually, subtly, the effects of your reflection walk will begin to take hold.

If you don't have a good place (i.e., pleasant and safe) to walk in your neighborhood or if the weather is rotten, have a backup walking plan in mind, such as the track, the gym, or the mall.

Exercise helps relieve stress, of course, and a reflection walk can help relieve stress and make you feel better about yourself at the same time.

First, put on comfortable walking shoes and comfortable clothes. Go to the front door and take five deep, full breaths, then say: "I'm ready to reflect upon all the good things in my life."

Out the door you go! Walk at a moderate pace—just fast enough to feel as though you are getting some exercise, but not enough to wear you out or make you frustrated or your muscles sore. As you walk, continue to take deep breaths. Most importantly, begin your mental list of all the things that are good about your life. Here are some questions you might consider:

- What is working?
- What parts of your life make you feel great?
- Who are the people in your life who make your life better?
- Whom do you love?
- What do you like about yourself?
- What are some of your fondest memories?
- Where do you love to go?
- What are your favorite things to do?
- What foods make you feel really good?
- What is your favorite book?
- What is it that you love about your home, your pets, your car, and/or your job?
- In what areas of your life are you successful?

CELEBRATE SUCCESSES

Don't undermine your own efforts at building up your self-esteem by telling yourself that an accomplishment isn't worth celebrating. If you, say, finally balanced the checkbook, or vacuumed, or turned off the TV last night earlier than you normally would have, that's great! Or maybe you didn't eat that bag of cookies or spend that $50 on stuff you don't need. You can and should feel good about things like that! So take 5 minutes each day and celebrate something that you did. You'll find that this quick, daily reminder of what you have accomplished will make you feel great about yourself!

CLEAN YOUR KITCHEN SINK

A clean sink has incredible stress-relieving power. The kitchen is the heart and soul of the house, and if one's house is symbolic of one's life (as it is in feng shui), then keeping the heart and soul in perfect order will resonate throughout your life.

If you aren't one of those people who has a hard time keeping things clean, this exercise isn't for you. But still, you may discover that the kitchen is a clear and direct reflection of how your life is going—when it sparkles, you feel great about yourself and everything in your life is working, but when it gets to the point that you won't let anybody into your kitchen, then chances are that your life is in disarray too.

The kitchen is a readymade jumping-in spot into life's stress cycles. No matter how busy you are, no matter how behind or over-whelmed you are, if you take just 5 minutes to go into your kitchen, fill the sink with hot soapy water, wash the rest of the dishes that are sitting around, and then drain the sink and scrub it down, you won't believe the impact doing that little bit of cleaning will have on your self-esteem.

Do this every day, especially every evening. The effect of waking up, walking into the kitchen, and seeing a bright, shiny sink—as opposed to a sink piled high with dirty dishes, making it impossible even to fill a teapot—will astound you. Really! This works.

The best part about getting into the habit of keeping your sink clean is that the rest of the kitchen will soon follow. And once you are in the habit of keeping your kitchen clean, it only takes a few minutes a day to keep it that way.

CLEAN OUT YOUR PURSE/WALLET

Organizing just one thing in your life can ease your stress considerably. Instead of watching TV tonight, why not tackle that purse that's been driving you crazy? Don't expect to do anything beyond this single area you've chosen. You'll be surprised how much better you'll feel once you've put a wallet or purse in order.

Throw away all the junk you don't need. File your receipts. Put everything in the right place. Flatten out your money and stack it so that all the bills face the same way. Clean out all the loose change and put it in a jar somewhere. (If you do this every day, you may soon have enough change in that jar to cover college tuition!)

DOODLE

Doodle! When something is worrying you and you find yourself obsessively trying to work out a logical solution, give your left brain a break and let your right brain exercise for a while. Doodling taps your creative side, balancing out an overworked brain. Your creative side just might come up with the solution you've been scrambling for!

When you are in a stressful situation, take 5 minutes to stop and doodle. It doesn't matter if you don't know how to draw—doodles are not meant to be judged, analyzed, or displayed. This is work that comes directly from your subconscious. It is a process of releasing what you are holding onto, mentally, deep inside. And that feels good.

TAKE A BREAK

To give yourself a break and help keep a leash on your frustration and stress, take this special 5-minute time-out for yourself.

1. Lean back against a wall and press the back of your body toward the wall. Feel supported by the wall. Focus on your breath.
2. Try to observe the flow of emotions. See if you can identify what emotion is present. Breathe into the emotion to see what is happening right now.
3. Take a few more breaths. Consider: what is the best way to handle your current stressful situation?

When you come to a place of peace and insight, rejoin the situation. Trust that you will know what to do. As you come to a place of calm, other people will feel it too (even if they only feel it on a subconscious level), and they will begin to feel calm as well.

PRACTICE PERFECTION MEDITATION

No matter what your so-called faults may be by worldly standards (or by your own standards), you are a perfect spirit inside. Here is a meditation to help you realize it.

1. Sit or lie comfortably and close your eyes.
2. Relax and focus on your breathing. Then, every time you exhale, imagine breathing out all the negativity inside you.
3. Every time you inhale, imagine breathing in pure, white light that fills you with positive energy.
4. As you breathe, repeat the word *perfection* out loud or to yourself. As you say the word, know that it describes you.

SAY "OH, WELL"

When you feel a rage, a surge of irritation, a flood of despair, a panic, or a fit of yelling coming on, one way to circumvent the surge is to consciously adopt a passive attitude. You may not always be able to stop and meditate, find a quiet place, focus on a mantra (a word or sound you repeat while meditating that helps clear and center your mind, bringing a feeling of peace), or even get comfortable, but you can adopt a passive attitude. How? Two words: Oh, well.

These two little words are extremely powerful. Really! Someone criticizes you? Oh, well. You spilled your coffee on your keyboard? Oh, well. Something is broken, wrecked, ruined? Oh, well. Your child talks back? Oh, well.

This response may seem wrong to you. Oh, well? Won't that keep you from learning from your mistakes? Won't that encourage people to walk all over you? Certainly not. If your child talks back to you, that doesn't mean he or she shouldn't have to suffer the consequences, but it also doesn't mean you have to get all worked up about it. Besides, a serene parent doling out consequences is much more in control than a flustered parent.

If you make a mistake, learn from it. Something happened. You'll be more careful next time. But "Oh, well" means you recognize that attaching negative emotions to a mistake will cloud your thinking rather than clear it. If you aren't filled with rage, you'll be better able to respond and react appropriately. You'll calmly and politely respond to the client. You'll calmly clean your keyboard rather than throwing the whole computer against the wall. You'll write a sincere and heartfelt letter of apology to your grandmother that isn't stained with tears. You'll buy your own tube of toothpaste rather than get irritated with your partner for leaving the cap off.

"Oh, well" can become a mantra of its own, reminding you at the onset of your stress reaction to let go of the stressful part of the experience. It doesn't mean you ignore the experience itself—it means you stop your body from damaging itself with a surge of unnecessary stress hormones. Unless you need to fight or flee, you're better off without that cortisol surge.

So relax. Say "Oh, well." You're balancing your stress response with a relaxation response.

RETHINK THE "TREAT"

Some people eat pretty well some of the time but can't get over the notion that on special occasions or when they've had a hard day, they deserve a treat. If you are one of those people, you can rethink the "treat" concept.

It is so easy to eat in response to stress. Many people do it. After all, don't you deserve it? Don't you deserve a treat?

Sure you do. But a treat doesn't have to be about food. Take 5 minutes from your day and brainstorm some possible treats for yourself. If you have a list in your mind, you will be less likely to reach for food in a weak moment. A treat could be a movie, a day trip, a full hour of doing nothing, a visit to the salon, a game of golf in the middle of the afternoon, letting yourself go to bed at nine p.m. There is so much that is wonderful, fun, and rewarding in life that has nothing to do with food! Get in the habit of thinking creatively about how to reward yourself.

And if you just have to reward yourself with food, make it absolutely worth the indulgence. A little bit of something superb is a far more rewarding and sensual experience than a whole lot of low-quality anything! A single piece of the highest-quality imported chocolate, a thin slice of cake and a tiny cup of espresso from the best dessert café in town, a small but perfect filet mignon wrapped in the best bacon... Whatever your indulgence is, savor every bite—and don't do anything else while you're enjoying your treat.

TRY FRIEND THERAPY

Treating your stress with friend therapy doesn't mean you sit at home alone and wait for your friends to come to you. It means you take the initiative and get out there to make contact with your friends. Sometimes it just takes a few minutes and a few words to find someone who is in the same position as you and needs friend therapy too.

Friend therapy isn't complicated. All it entails is human contact and not cyber contact (although cyber contact is better than no contact at all). Phone contact can be helpful, but nothing beats being physically present. Just being with another person and talking (even if it's not about your problems), having fun, and taking a break from the daily routine is a great way to relax, raise your self-esteem, and have the chance to be there for somebody else too. You don't have to do anything in particular with your friends to create friend therapy—you just have to build a social life.

TAKE "ME TIME"

"Me time" is just that: time that belongs solely to you. The idea sounds divine, but you've likely been inundated with things to do and running on automatic pilot for so long that you can't even imagine carving out time when no one else's needs take precedence. Unfortunately, like most people, you have so many things to do every day that you swim mindlessly through busy schedules, work responsibilities, piles of laundry, cooking, and cleaning. The hectic pace and endless list of demands are why you don't have time to experience what it feels like to be in your body when, oddly enough, that's exactly what you need. Taking precious moments throughout your day to revitalize and renew will make you a happier, healthier, and more patient person.

INDEX